Alexis Rhone Fancher's poems are bold and beautiful: D-cup titties in killer red stilettos, hesitant hearts consumed by wild weather, a hot G-spot marking the map of sensual liberation. Through titillation and imagination, Fancher's muses have climaxed together with the word, giving way to an explosion of bawdy delight.

    -- Rich Ferguson

Alexis Rhone Fancher's poetry is erotic, neurotic, kinetic, and never boring (this collection is multiple choice inclusive), but beyond all else, these are dangerous poems that surprise and threaten with the brazen flash of a stiletto (knives *and heels*, this collection is multiple choice inclusive). Just when you think you know where Rhone Fancher is going with a poem, she kidnaps its direction: thus, a torrid invitation for foreplay takes place inside Wayne's Volkswagen Repair Shop, a bruised memory of infidelity heals in the balm of forgiveness initiated by a pair of kinky boots working as the poem's operative metaphor, and a woman's recognition of her promiscuity gives rise to fierce bravada instead of shame: "Not the marrying kind./ I'm the fucking kind./ The lewd lingerie kind." These poems present an array of strong female voices, women who use their sexual prowess to wield great power--both in and out of the bedroom. Readers will recognize resonant echoes of Bukowski and Nin, two of Rhone Fancher's mentors, in this collection's commitment to desire and playfulness as counterpoints to human loneliness and despair. As tough, unshy, and sometimes as unflattering as these poems often are, at their best they are also honest and full of lyrical grace.

    --Tony Magistrale

This collection perfectly represents the brilliant meta-sexuality and diverse particularities of Alexis Rhone Fancher's work, not to mention its exuberance, flair, daring, and accompanying aesthetic tact. Equally devoted to the perfection of eye and ear in the harmonies of the photo and the poem, she is in process of taking these twin worlds by storm, without forfeiting the subtleties of a sophisticated playfulness…You will succumb to the cool contagion of such eroticism.

    -- Gerald Locklin

HOW I LOST MY VIRGINITY TO MICHAEL COHEN

and other heart stab poems

Alexis Rhone Fancher

Published by
Sybaritic Press
12530 Culver Blvd.
Suite 3
Los Angeles, CA 90066
www.sybpress.com

If you purchased this book without a cover you should be aware that this book is stolen property. It was reported as 'unsold and destroyed' to the publisher and neither the author nor the publisher has received payment for this 'stripped book.'

All work is Copyright 2014 by Alexis Rhone Fancher
Front cover photo and photo on p .36 (both photos of the author.) Both shot by Alan D. Miller
Back cover photo of author by Bob Abrams
All other photos by Alexis Rhone Fancher
p. 18, and p. 88 - Model: Lisa Thayer
p. 42, and p. 48 - Model: CLS Ferguson,
p. 80 - Model: Stella Kearney,

All rights reserved. No part of this book may be reproduced or transmitted in any form or by any means, electronic or mechanical, including photocopying, recording, or by any information storage and retrieval system without the written permission of the Publisher, except where permitted by law. For any information address: Sybaritic Press, Los Angeles, CA.

ISBN: 978-1-4951-2319-1
Printed in the United States of America
Second Edition
October 2014

Acknowledgements

Grateful acknowledgment is made to the editors of the following publications in which these works or earlier versions of them previously appeared: *A Story In 100 Words, Bare Hands Anthology, Bloom Literary Journal, BoySlut, Carnival Literary Journal, Chiron Review, Cliterature, Cultural Weekly, Deep Water Literary Journal, Downer Magazine, Fjords Review, FRE&D Journal, Gutter Eloquence Magazine, H_NGM_N, High Coupe, Little Raven, Luciferous, The Mas Tequila Review, Poeticdiversity, The Poetry Juice Bar, The Poetry Super Highway, rawboned, Tell Your True Tale,* "*Fierce Invalids: A Tribute To Arthur Rimbaud,*" edited by Glenn W. Cooper; "*From The Four-Chambered Heart - An Anthology for Anais Nin,*" edited by Marie Lecrivain; "*Storm Cycle 2013, The Best of Kind of A Hurricane Press,*" "*In Gilded Frame,*" and "*Poised In Flight*" anthologies, each edited by A.J. Huffman and April Salzano; "*Edgar Allan Poet Journal #2,*" edited by Apryl Skies; "*… and it happened under cover,*" edited by Alicia Winski and Rich Follett; "*THIS IS POETRY: Women of The Small Presses,*" edited by Michele McDannold; and "*WIDE AWAKE: The Pacific Coast Poetry Series*" forthcoming anthology of Los Angeles poets. Photos of the author by Alan D. Miller, except for back cover photo by Bob Abrams. All other photos are by the author.

Thank you to Chanel Brenner, Jack Grapes, Tony Magistrale, Cynthia Atkins, Michelle Bitting, Elya Braden, Marcus Elman, Tresha Faye Haefner, Bambi Here, Baz Here, Judi Kaufman, Adam Leipzig, Roz Levine, Gerald Locklin, Dr. Barbara Moreno, Kate O'Donnell, Wendy Rainey, Laurie Quinn Seiden, Lisa Thayer. Special thanks to Marie Lecrivain and Deborah L. Warner for believing in this collection. And thank you to my beloved Fancher, who knows me well, and loves me still.

for Fancher

Table of Contents

How I Lost My Virginity to Michael Cohen	1.
This is Not a Poem	3.
The First Time I Gave My Cousin Lisa an Orgasm	5.
Bad Girl	7.
Subterranean Lovesick Clues	11.
Five Urban Haiku	13.
Lust at the Cafe Formosa	15.
Love Bites	17.
Serial Wet Dreams in a '65 Mustang 289 Convertible	19.
I've Never Slept With a Mexican Before	21.
Takis, My Cypriot Lover	23.
Let's Be Happy Now	25.
I Want Louboutin Heels	27.
Handy	29.
Pretty Criminals	31.
Love Song for My Baby	33.
Perfect Mate	35.
Polaroid SX-70 Camera	37.
Property	39.
My First Homosexuals	41.
Happy Dick – A 100 Word Story	43.
The Best Bodies in L.A.	45.
The Best Crimes in L.A.	47.
The Best Hook-Ups in L.A.	49.
The Best Sex in L.A. (in the Summer)	51.
The Best Blondes in L.A.	53.
The Best Lays in L.A.	55.
The Happiest Men in L.A.	57.
At Twelve, The Awakening	59.
99-Seat Waver	61.
Territory	63.
Your Target	65.
Upon Running into My Ex on a Summer Afternoon	67.
Flashbacks	69.
Mayonnaise	71.
Alison L	73.

Underwater	75.
White Flag	77.
Staying Put	79.
When Two Poets Collide: For Anna	
After the Most Recent Breakup	81.
Like Sisyphus At the Chateau Marmont	83.
Rape Reality	85.
When	87.
The Narcissist's Confession	89.
Dos Gardenias	91.
At Last! Blues for Etta James	93.
Blackberry Haiku	95.
Walk All Over You	97.
La Petite Mort	99.
College Roommates	101.
Nebraska	103.
Dark Options	105.
Pick Up – A 100 Word Story	107.
Something I Want to Tell You	109.
Second Chances	111.
White People's Problems	113.
All the Rumors are True	115.
The Seven Stages of Love – An L.A. Haiku Noir Sequence	117.
Author Bio	119.

How I Lost My Virginity to Michael Cohen

1. My father hated him.
2. So his best friend, J.R., picked me up. Shook my daddy's hand at the door. Promised me back by midnight.
3. Daddy thought I was obedient, a good girl.
4. It was hot, even for August.
5. J.R.'s parents were in Vegas, so he loaned us their bedroom.
    5a.) They had a king-sized bed.
6. Diana Ross and The Supremes were singing Baby Love.
7. J.R. watched cartoons in the den.
8. Michael's middle finger furrowed between my thighs.
9. I felt that familiar wetness.
10. Except it wasn't my finger.
11. I remembered where I was and closed my eyes.
12. He pulled down my panties.
13. Pushed up my skirt.
14. No one had put their lips down there before.
15. No one.
16. It felt delicious.
17. I hoped he liked my scent.
18. There were lilies on the nightstand.
19. "Your hair smells so good," he mumbled.
20. He was holding his cock while he licked me.
21. I had never come before.
    21a.) Not like that.
22. It was then I knew I loved him.
23. He tasted like me.
24. His dick grew too big for my mouth.
25. When he entered me, it didn't hurt.
26. "I thought you were a virgin," he said.
27. I thought of the dildo that pleasured me in secret.
28. "Horseback riding," I said.
29. When the rubber broke, he promised he wouldn't come inside me.
30. He promised.

This is Not a Poem

This is NOT a poem. Bam! This is an assault to your senses, a rape of your status quo. This is NOT a poem, not some trendy leopard print, not a polka dot parade. No. You do not smell hot dogs, cotton candy or frankincense. The myrrh has left the building. This is NOT a poem. It's an anthem, a declaration of noncompliance, a liberation proclamation. Snap! Snap! This is NOT a poem. It's a love song, a torch song, a song of myself and NOT you. No tears, got it? Don't act like a girl. Blow your nose wipe your eyes. Don't make yourself look stupid! This is NOT a poem. It's salt poured on the wound. Can it feel? Only if I let it burn too deeply. This is NOT a poem. No! It isn't good enough. No. I've read poems & it's not the same. Snap! Snap! This is NOT a poem. It's a hip hop of my own creation, a celebration of my brains my breasts my underground caverns. This is NOT a poem. It's a rite of passage, a starry night, a reluctant homage to your name, spelled out in lonely Broadway lights. My life goes dark without you, honey. Clap! Clap! This is NOT a poem. You with your lust, with your X-ray eyes. Listen up now. Be careful how you love me; be grateful for second chances. Don't push too hard. I might surprise you. You'll see, I'm tougher than I look: I eat Bukowski for breakfast.

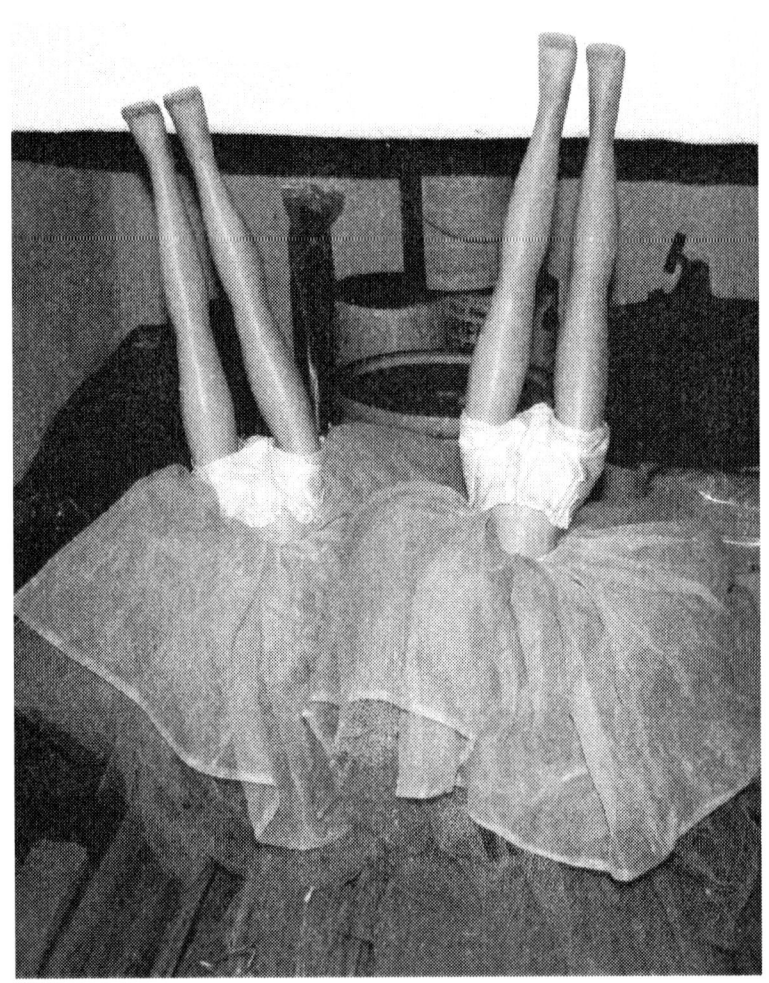

The First Time I Gave Cousin Lisa an Orgasm

We'd been playing doctor for months by then,
her huge breasts a magnet, her soft mons

a refuge from my impending adolescence. Some
nights, unable to dream, I'd touch myself like Lisa,

replay the us, hidden between twin beds in her pink,
froufrou bedroom, my aunt across the hall, making dinner,

the door half open, my fingers three thick in her daughter's
pussy, the pin point of Lisa's nipple stuffed in my mouth.

I'd suck. She'd moan. I'd explore. She'd explode.
It was the most powerful I'd ever be.

The first time I made cousin Lisa come
we looked into each other's aloneness; the boys

who didn't want us yet, the girls who shunned us
like they saw something we didn't.

When I let myself remember, here's what I see:
me, on my knees, between the beds,

the bounty of Lisa spread before me
like a feast, her steady rocking against my wrist

a sharp pleasure, the rug burn that my knees endured
a penance, prepaid.

Bad Girl

He could smell thrill seeker
all over me.
But he wasn't like the others.
Tenderness so foreign, confusing.
He caressed me like I mattered,
kissed away all my misgivings,
breathed me in.
"Is this what you want?" he asked.

Subterranean Lovesick Clues

1.
I remember listening
to Bob Dylan in Donna Melville's attic
bedroom, 3 a.m. We were
drinking her daddy's bourbon, playing
Subterranean Homesick Blues over and over,
memorizing it word by mumbled word.
*Johnny's in the basement,
mixing up the medicine, I'm on the pavement, thinkin' 'bout
the government...* Donna passed me the bottle. The bourbon made
me sick but I took a swig anyway. I didn't want her to think I was a
lightweight. The word might get
around.

Maggie comes fleet foot, face full of black soot...

Donna took the bottle to her lips, her moon face flushed,
beautiful. She was my first Catholic, and I was in
awe of the certainty of her faith, couldn't take my eyes off
the lucky gold crucifix that dangled between her breasts.

"What do you think *Freewheelin'* means?"
We were on the bed, pretending to study
the album cover, Dylan and some blond on
a New York street, looking happy. "I think it means fuck the
consequences, just do what you want," I said.
Drunk, reckless, soon I'm ready to do what I want -
let my hand slip from the
album jacket to Donna's left breast. Her sharp intake of breath. My
tom-tom heart.

Look out kid, it's somethin' you did God knows when but you're doin' it again...

These were the moments I lived for at 13: the hot, disheveled solace
of Donna's attic room, her clueless family asleep below,
Dylan's growl on the stereo,

Donna in my arms, her lips on mine, her tongue down my throat,
Fingers fumbling with my zipper.

2.
Get dressed get blessed try to be a success...

3.
Donna hits the Confessional.
"Father, forgive me for I have sinned."

I am that sin. I listen in.

"I kissed a girl," says my girl.
"You'll go to hell," says the desiccated
man in the box.

4.
light yourself a candle...
you can't afford the scandals...

5.
The Gospel According To St. Donna:

She is the innocent,
I am the sin.
I am the bad girl
That let the sin in.

6.
I remember listening
to Bob Dylan in Donna Melville's attic
bedroom, 3 a.m., the last time I drank
her daddy's bourbon, the last time we ever touched.
This was the moment I dreaded at 14: afraid of
the spark, afraid of her own ignition -
Donna changed the rules.
Jesus had entered the bedroom.

"See ya," Donna said as she walked me
out of her life.
"Soon?" I asked. (A girl can dream, right?)
"Sure," she said.

7.
She didn't call.
I didn't call back.

You don't need a weather man to know which way the wind blows...

Five Urban Haiku

Haiku For My Beloved
I ask for breakfast,
Instead, he brings me flowers.
Am I still hungry?

He Searches For Reasons
material girl?
that was your complaint, right? Like
a car's a bad thing?

The Plot Thickens
Once betrayed, twice shy.
Says he's not that kind of guy.
Should I believe him?

Cruel Haiku To A Former Lover
there's a touch of the
poet in everyone - well,
everyone but you.

How The Artist Sees The World
It's about the light.
How it slants entire worlds
With its opinion.

Lust at the Cafe Formosa

Once, at the Cafe Formosa in L.A.,
I saw the most beautiful girl. And the
best part was, you could see she didn't know it. Yet.
Didn't know how anxiously her nipples strained
against her shirt, or that her endless legs
and sloe-eyed gaze were worth a million
bucks... to someone.

She was a sway-in-the-wind willow, her skin the
pale of vanilla ice cream, her hair all shiny black
straight like an Asian girl's, thick as a mop.
She was maybe seventeen, on the brink, so ripe sex
exuded from her pores. She leaned against the juke box,
fingering those quarters in her shorts' pocket so
they jingled like Christmas, the fabric between
her thighs stretched to bursting.

When her food arrived, the girl unwrapped the
chopsticks, lifted Kung Pow chicken to her mouth,
inhaled the spicy morsels. A long, sauce-slicked
noodle played with her lips and I longed to lick it off.
I'd been alone four years by then, so
used to it, even the longing had long departed.

Then she showed up, all fresh-spangled, clueless.
If I didn't walk out then I never would. Elvis was
crooning *Don't Be Cruel*, but I knew she would be.
Girls like her can't help it.

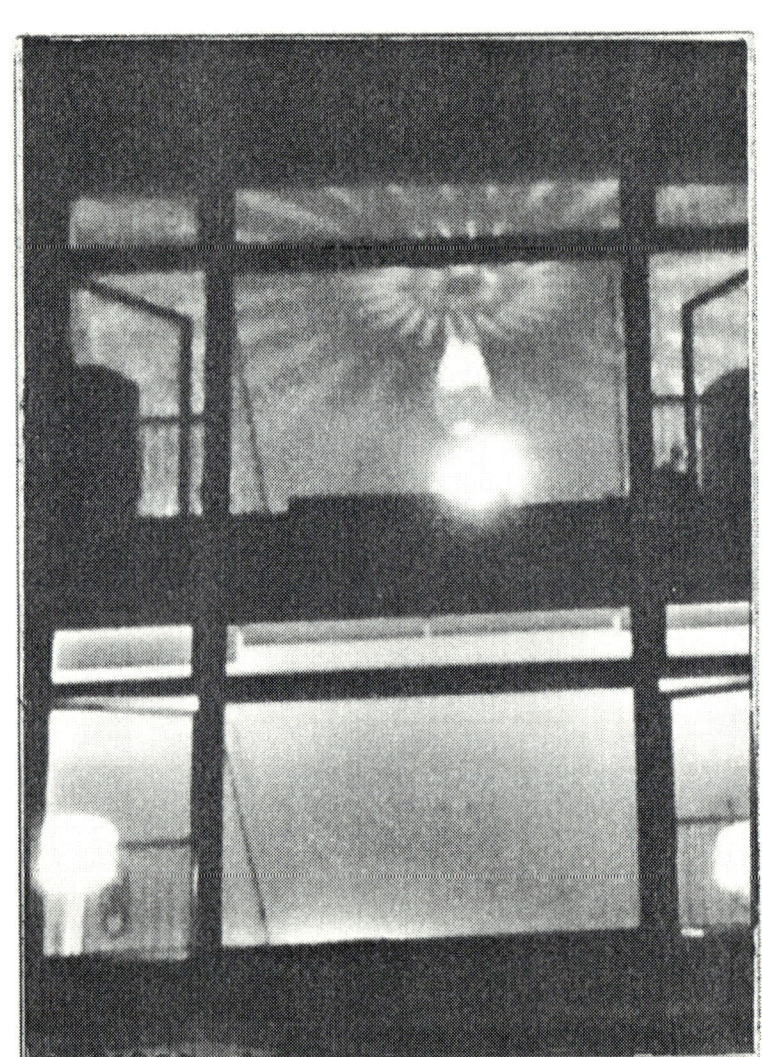

Love Bites

Love is not divine.
Your addiction.
And mine.

Your lips, dining on
my bare shoulder,
your hands claiming
my breasts.

When I desire you,
I think: Swallowed up.
Disappeared. Your fingers
at my throat. Your teeth
sunk into my flesh.

Why is that sexy?

I get all mixed up.

When I desire you,
I think: no strings.

Like that's a good thing.

You've got my number.

This time, try not to
leave marks.

Serial Wet Dreams in a '65 Mustang 289 Convertible

always a stick shift
black leather seats
black like
the stockings
the boots
the man

always September
midnight, full moon
ass on the slide
driver's side
no panties
no problem

my girlfriend
always said I
was a switch hitter

what now? he asked
(as he) snapped the
handcuffs
on my wrists
put the car in park

it was as far away
from Daddy
as I could
get.

I'd Never Slept With a Mexican Before

ON THE ROAD
I had a knife with me that day,
I don't know why.

We just started driving upstate.
When I asked where we were going
he said, "Coffee."

He was too short for me anyway.

In my dream there was poison in the coffee.
It tasted sweet. I didn't seem to mind.

IN THE DINER
There were miles between us,
a Sahara.

"It's okay to smoke," he said.
"As long as you're not a train."

When he reached for my hands
I saw tattooed saints on his wrists
where the long sleeves shortened.

He let go like he'd been burned.

Folded. A barricade. A moat.

I fondled the knife in my purse
till he caught my eye.

"Keep 'em where I can see 'em."

I could live with that.

IN THE MOTEL
We danced in the open space
between the queen bed and the door.
He sweated through his button down,
a silver crucifix at his throat,
looked like Mark Anthony
in the motel marquee's light.

Free Cable. Free Ice. No Vacancy.

He kicked off his pants, turned out the light.
Fucked me with his shirt on.

IN THE MORNING
I surprised him in the shower,
saw his tattooed glory, sleeves,
the American eagle
full-winged across his chest,
"Semper Fi" emblazoned on a
ribbon in its mouth.

I threw the knife out the window
once the car passed Santa Barbara.

"The road is the journey," he said,
the sin of regret in his eyes.

Takis, My Cypriot Lover

My Cypriot Lover

is probably dead by now.
men don't live long in that
part of the world. there's
always some cause worth the
dying.

My G-Spot

I never knew,
he said. in a land of shrouded,
voiceless women, I
cried out, raked my
nails to blood
across his back, arching
yielding
into him, couldn't get
enough of him

he had let loose
a lunatic. a woman who
came at the least
provocation, who
spread her legs,
showed him the mystery.

oh, the infinite power
of his up-close investigation,
my wetness slathered all over
his smile.

My Regrets

a lifetime later, and sometimes
I still think of him when I come.

oh, Takis! black-haired Adonis,
eyes the blue of the Adriatic.
did you ever find another like me?
or did you spend your whole life searching?

Let's Be Happy Now!

Danny looks at me, the way
they all do:
lust-eyes. He waylays me in the
bathroom, hairy arms suddenly
around my waist.
"I heard U fucking Mickey last night,"
he says, "heard U cry out,
& no, no
it wasn't a cat but it yowled,
U yowled and my dick got hard, baby.
U know U want it. Deny it & I'll call U a
fucking liar.
I don't care who we hurt!
Let's be happy now!"

I confess,
his recklessness holds a certain allure,
& then I'm fuckin' him real high &
hard, up against the sink in the
bathroom, with his soon-to-be
wife just outside,
ear pressed against the door.
Not the marrying kind.
I'm the fucking kind.
The lewd lingerie kind.
The girl you
bring home for the
weekend,
not to meet the family
kind.
The dirty little secret,
the girl you jack off to after your
wife
goes to sleep.
The one you think about
so you can get it up with the
old lady,

year after year,
decade after dreary
decade. The one you wish you'd married
& you'd be happy now,
happy now,
so very happy,
now.

I Want Louboutin Heels

I want Louboutin
heels with those trademark red soles,
I want them sexy, I want them high.
I want them slingback and peep-toed
so I can flash the purple polish
on my tootsies. I
want to wear them out of the store, just
you try and stop me.

I want to wow them on
Washington, saunter past C&O Trattoria
and Nick's Liquor Mart, those bottles of Stoli
stacked in the window, calling my name, past the
summer-clad tourists in December, shivering,
barefoot, like L.A. has no winter.

In those shoes I'm hot,
stop-a-truck hot, prettiest
girl in school hot, and this
time, I know it.
Flaunt it. Hell, I own it. In those shoes I can
pick and choose, not settle for some loser.
Not drink away regrets, pound back Stoli at
Chez Jay's, flash their scarlet bottoms when I kneel.

I'll wear them like flesh,
like hooves, like sin.
I'll keep their secrets, won't spill
where they've been.

Better those shoes with their lurid soles
than you with yours.

Handy

I wanted you small and folded
in my pocket. Like a Swiss Army knife.
Like a blow up doll. I wanted you
to fuck me and then disappear.

You wanted me wide open,
surrendered. Like a vacation.
Like a ripe nectarine.

I wanted to use you for sex.
Isn't that what all
men dream of?

You wanted to fuse us to the
bed, glue me, on my hands
and knees, to the sheet, through
the mattress, tether me to the box
springs, nail me through
the floor.

It scared me out the door.

That day I saw you in Venice,
you walked past me
like your cock had
never been in my mouth.

I almost grabbed a fistful of you,
crammed you in like food.

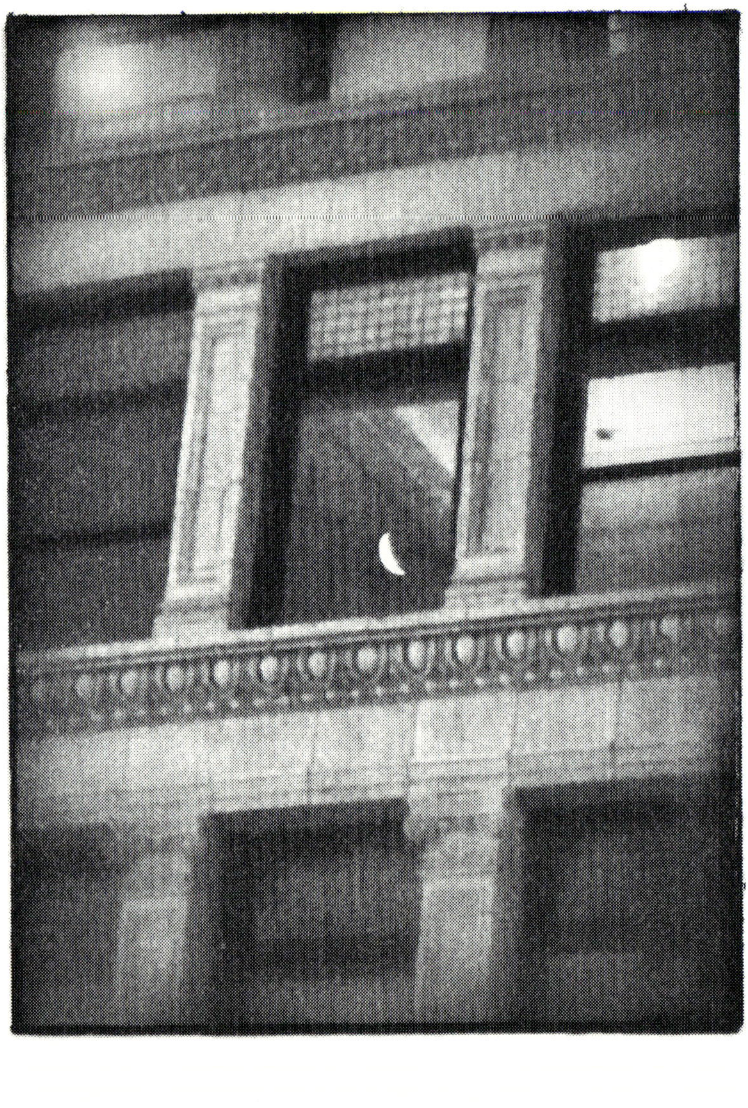

Pretty Criminals
(Reading Rimbaud On Broadway. in Downtown Los Angeles)

I. A tall girl waits beneath an awning, shivering,
the unconscious sway of her hips an invitation.
It's November, but she has no coat,
only great presence and a dreamy look.
She is waiting for someone.
She is seventeen and not really serious.

Il pleut des cordes.

On clear nights they'd stroll these streets
beneath the neon moon, whispering snippets from
Rimbaud's *Illuminations*, her kiss on his lips
a fluttering, living thing.

II. The tall girl scans the 5 p.m. crowd, escaping.
Broadway suddenly full-up, the skies still teeming,
the rain gutters' swell surprisingly sexual. She feels
a pull in her heart, and steps from under the awning,
ventures into the street in her little ankle boots, the
sound buds in her ears blasting Vivaldi.

Young, reckless, so heedless of her own safety!
She's only looking for him, not the car on rain-slicked
pavement careening toward her. Is it just dumb luck
that he appears at that moment and snatches her from death?

Now he thinks he owns her.
No one can tell him she's bad news. Fickle. Seventeen.

III. When they make their desperate love, isolated in a doorway,
infused with the celebration of death defied, oblivious
of the crowds, the rain, the future, can their ancient savagery
ever be forgiven, these pretty criminals,
whimpering in the mud of the street?

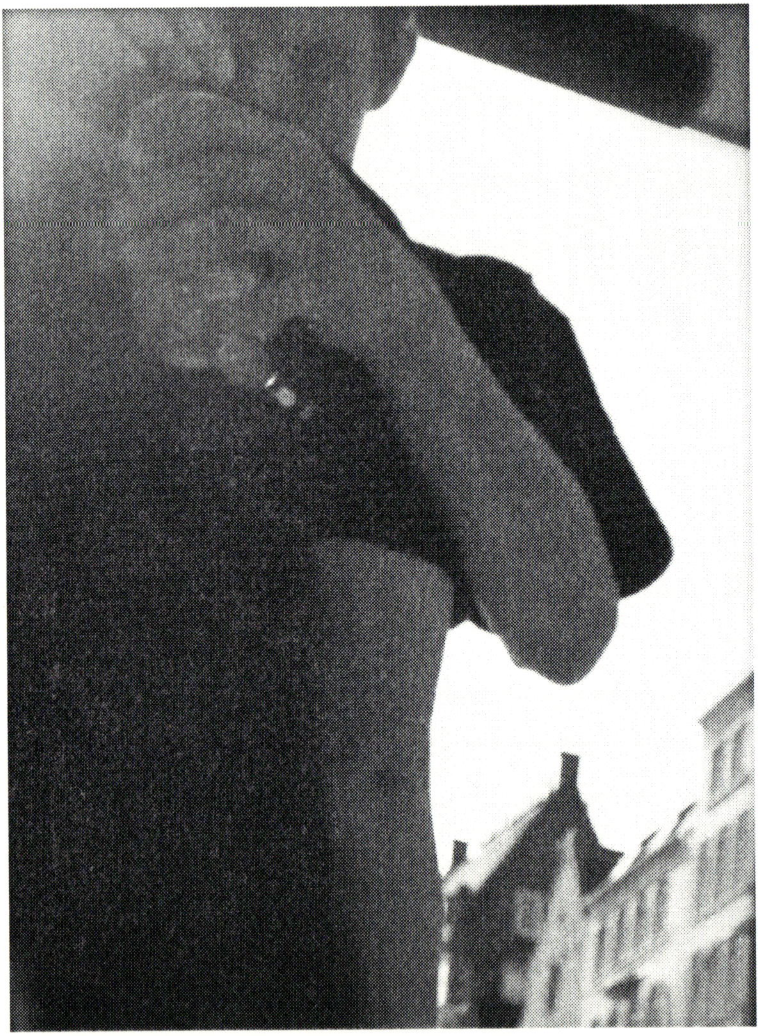

Love Song for My Baby

If I could catch my breath I'd suck your cock but I'm so overcome by your studly chest, your hairy thighs, your endearingly bony knees that I'm afraid I'd choke on it. Anyway, forget the preliminaries, I just want to jump your bones, throw a saddle over your rump and ride, pony, ride. I want to blog on your biceps, write erotica on your elbows, I want to tattoo my memoirs on your ass. I want to lead you out of the stable, trot you around, give you your head, then rein you in. I want you to taste the bit in your mouth, and have it taste sweet like Tic Tacs, like summer time, like ginger-ale. Just like you taste to me. I want to corral you in my arms, square dance in the moonlight, dos-si-dos with the best of 'em. I could put you on the stage in Tijuana. That donkey's dick's got nothing on you, babe. *Nada. Niet. Rien.* My very own John Holmes. I woke yesterday in a pool of you and me. Your lips fastened on my pussy, your hot breath steaming up my thighs. You were humming the theme from Dr. Zhivago and the dark buzz made my clitty hard as a little dick. So kiss me already, and then let's stick it in. This is L.A., for Chrissakes, and the livin' is on the beach, on the fly, on the installment plan. Wanna know how I see it? Each of us teeters on the totter, a paycheck away from homeless, from ruin, just one pitch away from a shut-out, one sweet fuck away from the end.

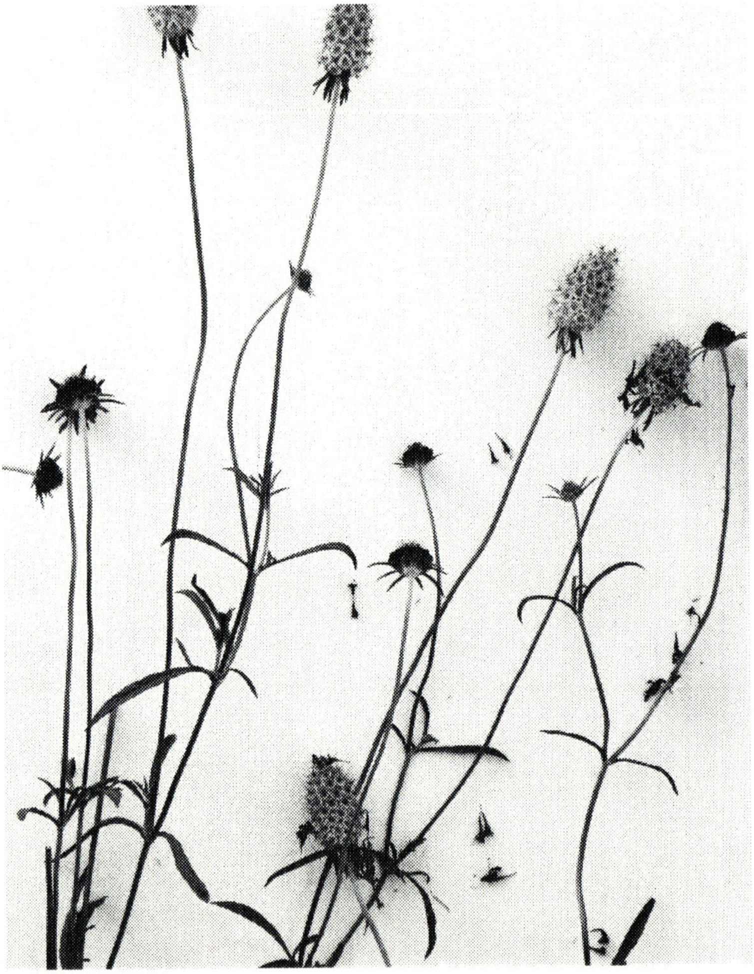

Perfect Mate

We make love, then spoon.
"Who's your favorite poet?" I ask,
expect he'll say Blake, Bukowski, Laux.
"Why you," he smiles, blue eyes
sparkling. How perfect to belong to
this man, who knows me so well, and
loves me still.

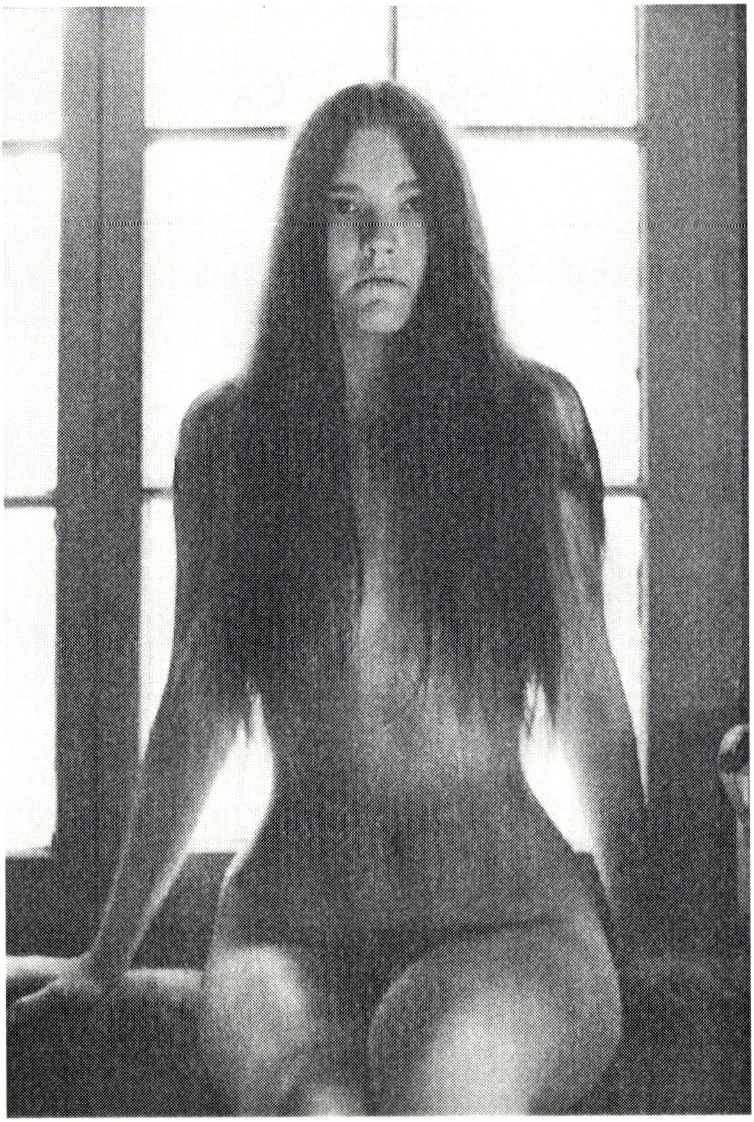

Polaroid SX-70 Land Camera

There's a reckless streak in me I can't control. It makes me do dangerous things. I know it's wrong, but I always fail, no willpower at all. The thing about Wayne, I tried to keep my distance, but he was hot, sexy in a middle-aged sort of way. He reminded me of some of my father's friends. I thought we were kindred spirits.

"I dream about you at night," he said, his voice husky, low. His breath smelled like clove gum and cigarettes. "I dream you do everything I tell you." He stepped into the small office in the back, came back with a Polaroid SX70, smiled and handed me the camera. "I want you to go into my office, pull down your panties, spread your legs and shoot a photo for me. You know what I want. Something really hot."

The phone rang. He picked it up. "Wayne's Volkswagen Repair." He turned back to me, leering. "I'll make it worth your while," he said.

I sat on the cold metal stool at the counter, legs crossed, black skirt riding up my thighs. It was a long way from Shangri La. Fenders and transmissions littered the floor, tools hung on pegs nailed into the walls, and half-rebuilt engines balanced on benches and worktops. Every surface was covered with a layer of greasy dust that mingled with Wayne's ever-present cigarette and made the air heavy and hard to breathe. What was it about these sleazy places? I felt sick. My stomach bottomed out with that familiar, crazy swirling. Sickening, but I still craved it. Bad girl with a bad habit. Very, very bad.

I clutched the camera, watched the dust particles swirl in the light shafts from the open door. I could leave, follow the light right out to Lakewood Blvd. Get away this time, before I got in past my depth. Instead, I looked inside to where the light ended, where it spotlighted the Rigid Tool calendar with a naked "Miss July" hanging in the place of honor behind the cash register. Someone had given her a mustache. My head hurt from the loud banging, rhythmic, like a clock striking, going all the time. Wayne's two Mexicans pounded metal out back, competing with 40 mph traffic on the street. The Golden Oldies station blared out the hits.

I couldn't hear myself think except to think that Wayne was waiting for an answer. To think that I should get out now, be that lady my mother raised me to be. Cold hands. Cold heart. My mother. I could never tell her, she'd never understand about this. About why I do this. Over and over! About how crazy I get around the wrong kind of man, a man like Wayne, so crazy when he smoothed his black hair back from his face and wiped the sweat on his greasy jeans. Slumming, that's what she'd call it.

But me, I never listened, I was too busy dreaming about how his blue work shirt was half unbuttoned. I could see the thick hair on his chest and the pocket of his shirt that said "Wayne" in big red letters. Crazy for his smell, his hands, big hands, calloused, black in the creases. I wondered what they'd feel like on my skin. I wondered what he meant by "I'll make it worth your while."

Wayne looked right at me as he hung up the phone. "Well," he said. "What's it gonna be?"

Property

1. In the light
I keep thinking about the way
you keep your thumb hooked in
the belt loop of my jeans, like you have me on
a leash, like you own me. I'm not sure I don't like it.

2. In the dark
I lie on top, your skin grazes mine. I breathe
your scent, burrow in your flesh, forehead
flush against your belly, eager
mouth fellating your cock. So this is love!

3. In the even darker
Go ahead. Push me
down. Pin my wrists. Wedge your knees between my
thighs; pry me open. You know
you want to explore my corridor, my
antechamber, my presidential suite. There's a basket
of fruit on my D-cup titties, Veuve Cliquot in my fridge.

4. In the winter
You like fucking on top of the sheets, heater off,
windows open to remind us we're still breathing. I
can see your breath, its smoke - and mirrors.

5. In the cut
I keep thinking about the way
you keep me under your thumb.
"Yes," you say. "This *is* love."
And I'm not sure I don't like it.

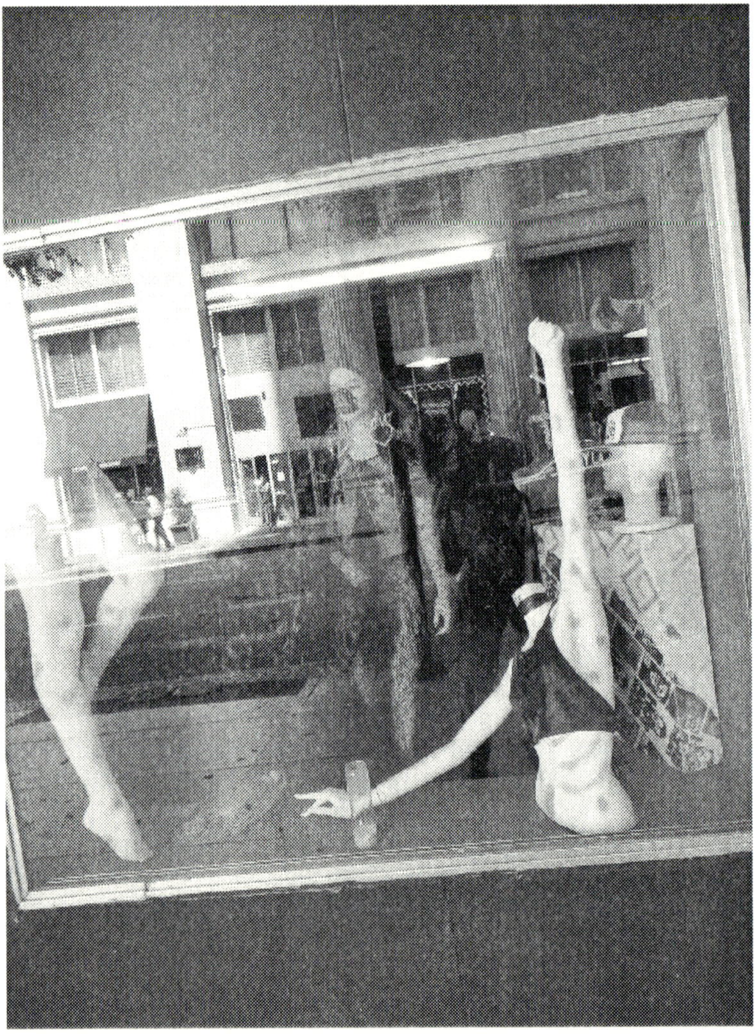

My First Homosexuals

After I put my foot in
I see white spunk, floating
on the surface. At the deep
end, Joe and Elliott conspire.
Heads too close together. It
makes me feel queer.

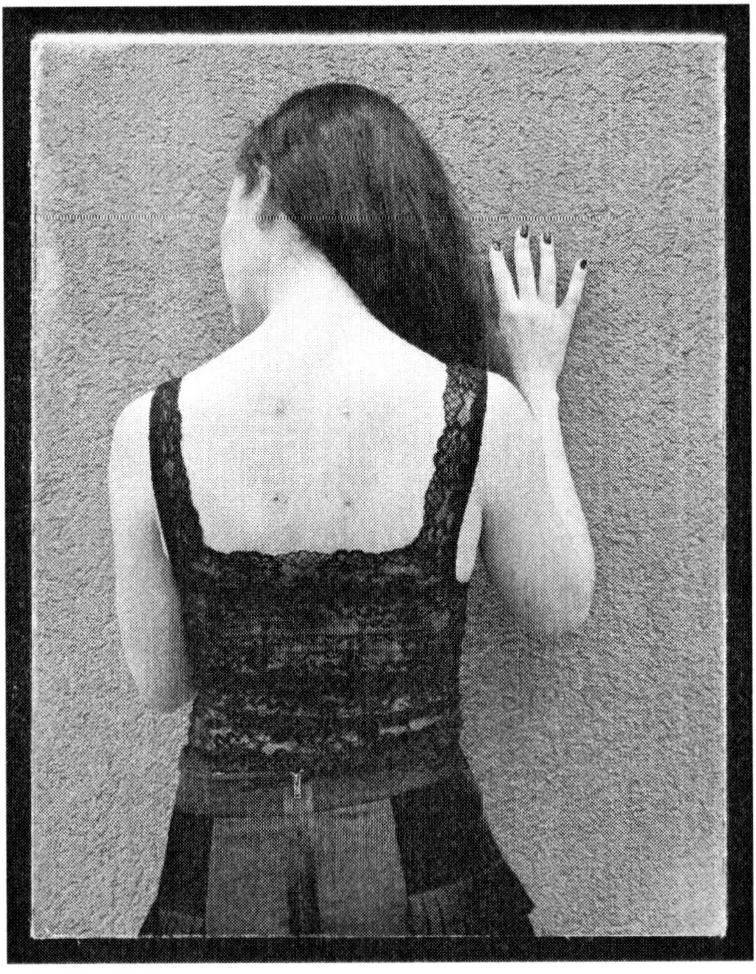

Happy Dick - A 100 Word Story

I fell hard for Johnny Carvello. Dagos got me wet. He preferred strippers, ringside tables, hand on crotch, watching them work the pole. Called it "happy dick." We were the perfect pair, the ex-Mafioso and the car crash cripple. Both, second-rate goods. He had a thing for my still-perfect feet, bathed them in rosewater, sucked the toes, jacked himself off all over them. He'd pose me naked, on the bed, do tai chi by candlelight, his eyes on mine. Months into it when he tried to fuck me, I broke it off. The relationship, not the dick.

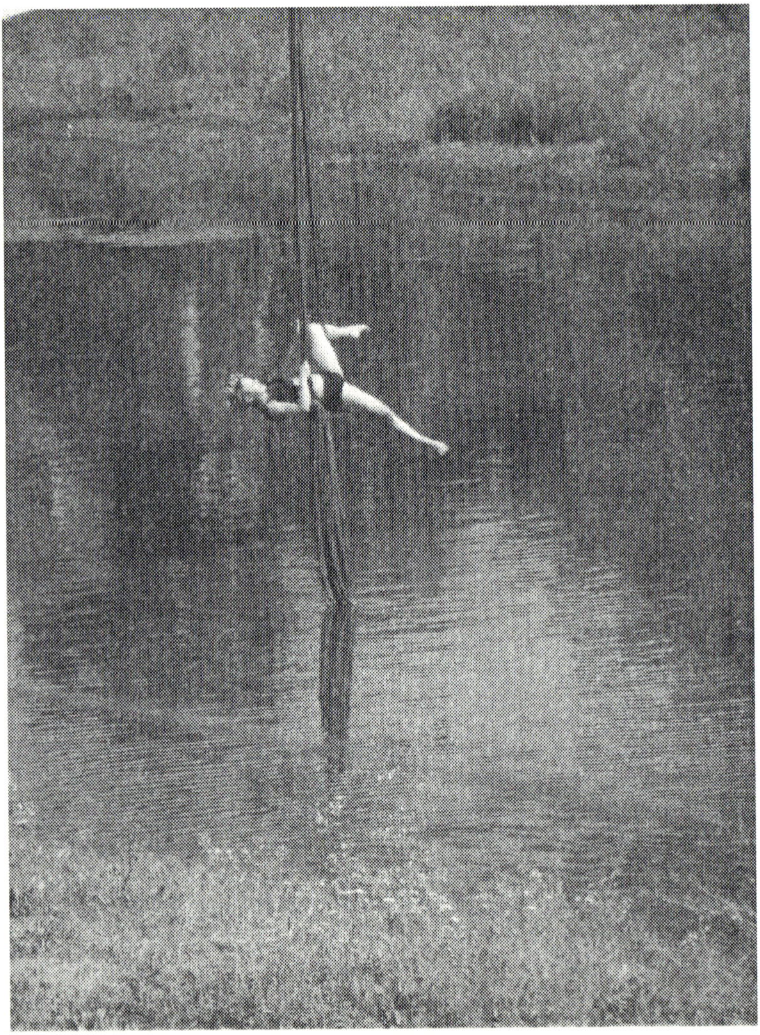

The Best Bodies in L.A.

are from Topanga Canyon. Also,
some parts of the Palisades,
hot women who shop
in Malibu, who do Pilates
and like to sweat, like them
younger, like to pretzel
in bed, gymnast-lean,
stick their landing every time.

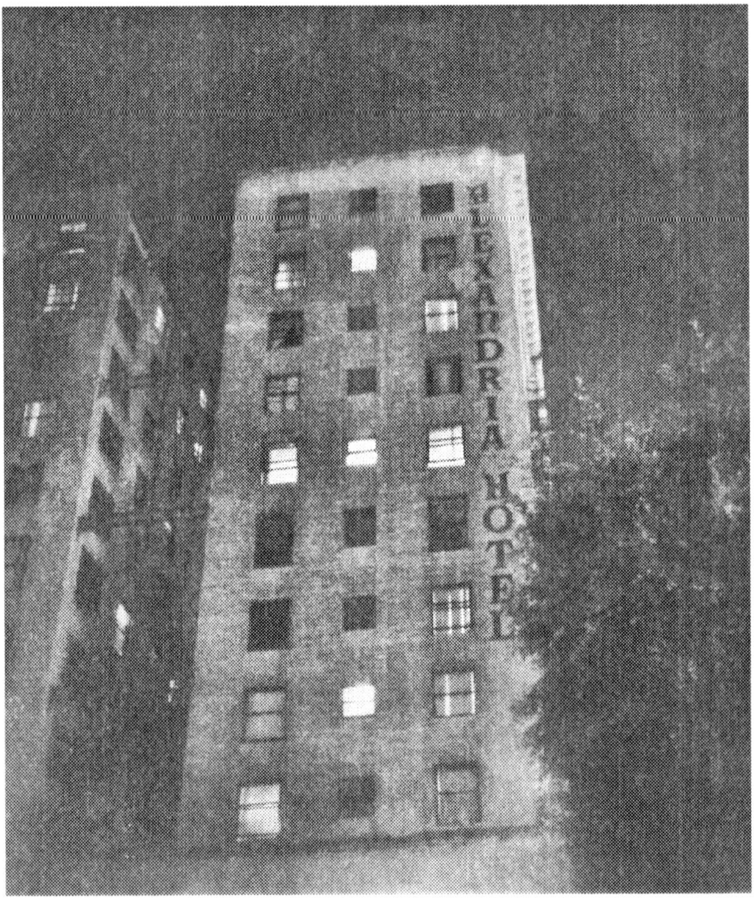
HOTEL

The Best Crimes in LA

are crimes of the heart, both wrists
tied to the bedpost, shame checked
at the door. His technique was
perfected long before he got
to me, stupid girl, eyes shut,
legs wide open, welcoming
the thief of hearts, this man who
breaks his wild wife like a horse.

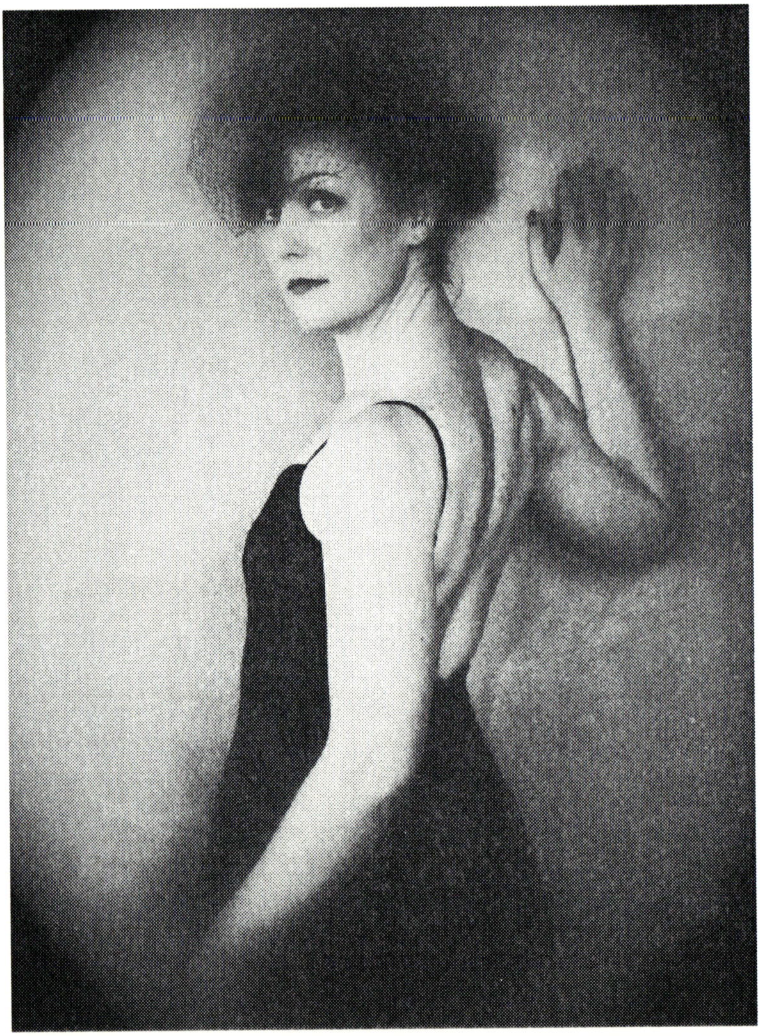

The Best Hook-Ups in L.A.

work construction, on the look-out
for neglected housewives. "Just
begging for it," he tells
his friends. "A drunk fuck against the wall
in back, doesn't count,"
she tells her husband. "3 bottles,
an oxy. I was seduced,"
she tells her friends, "by a butt-crack."

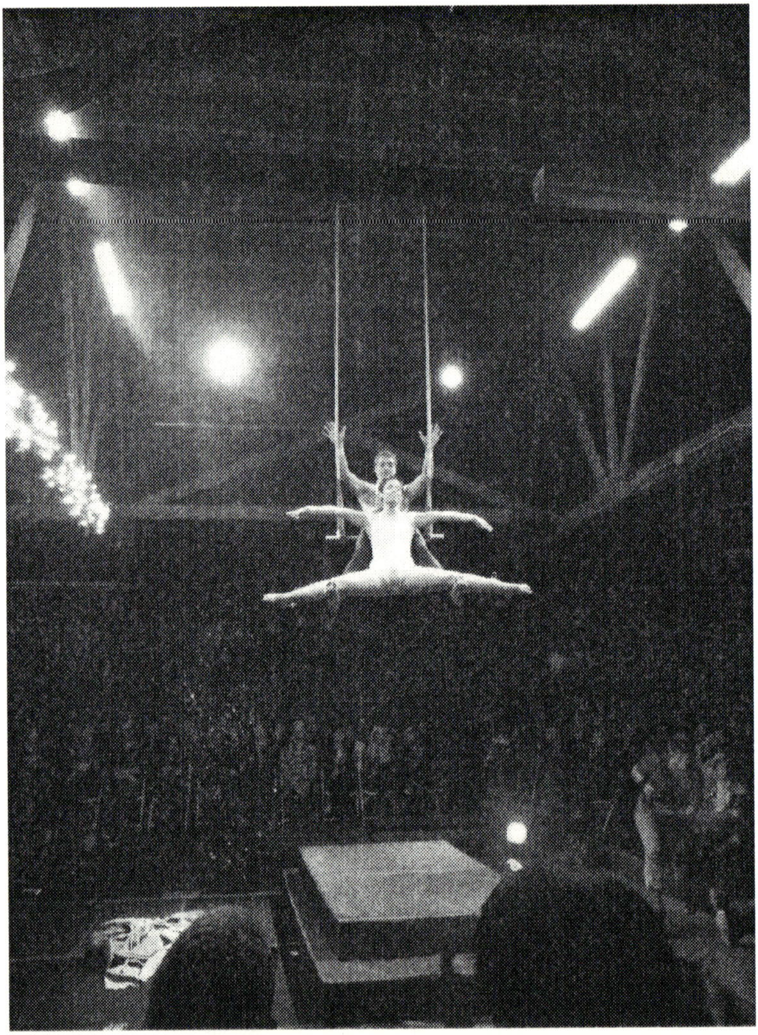

The Best Sex in L.A. (Is In Summer)

after sunset, when the frantic
heat surrenders to a cool,
hip breeze. Desert-dwellers
revive in neon, like to sip chilled
martinis, like to
get naked, like to fuck in the
dark: heartless, anonymous
and far less likely to sweat.

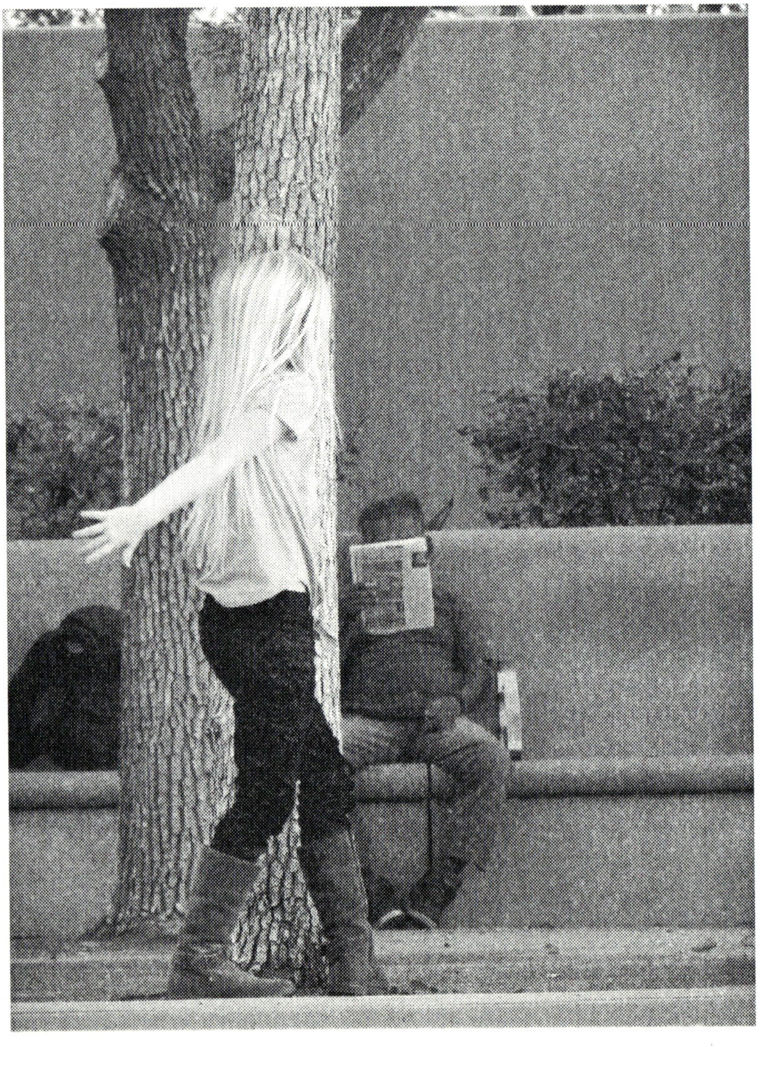

The Best Blondes in L.A.

stroll Rodeo Drive, on the prowl
for music execs, lawyers,
not actors, (subject to
reversal of fortune, on the street
at cancellation).
no. money talks and a girl has
a short shelf life. no one said
stupid was a hair color.

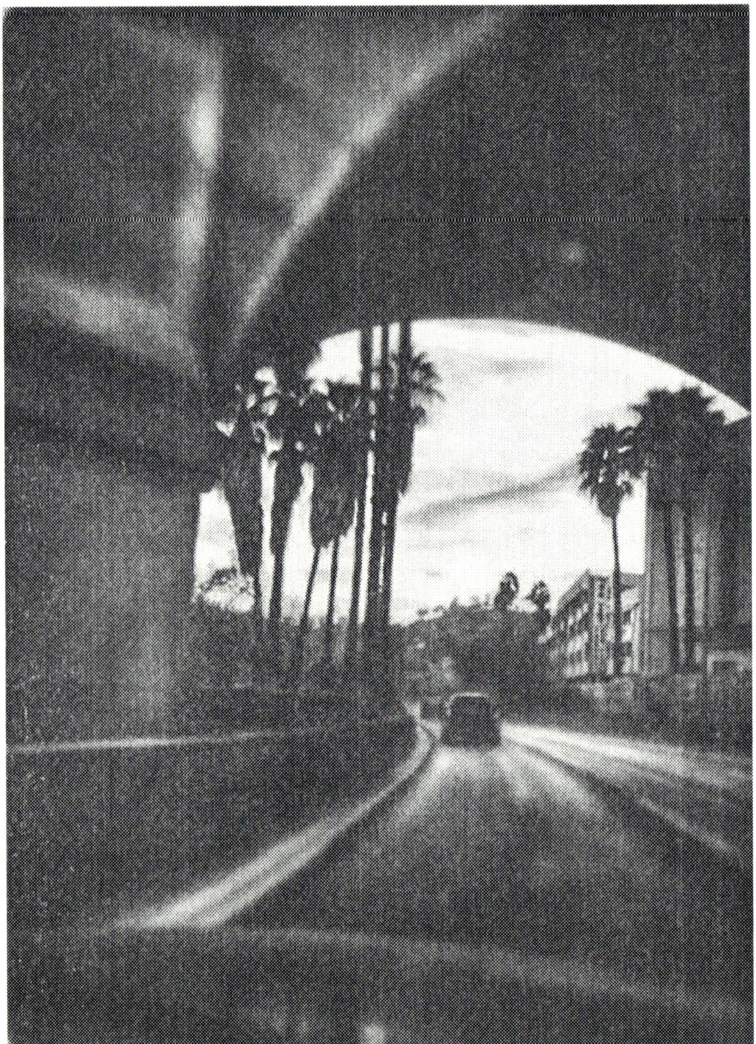

The Best Lays in L.A.

are photographed on Venice Beach,
sunbathe topless, silicone
tits defying gravity.
I don't want to be a model or
a 48 DD. Too much weight.
Too much responsibility.
But oh! the accidental brush of
his fingers across my nipple.

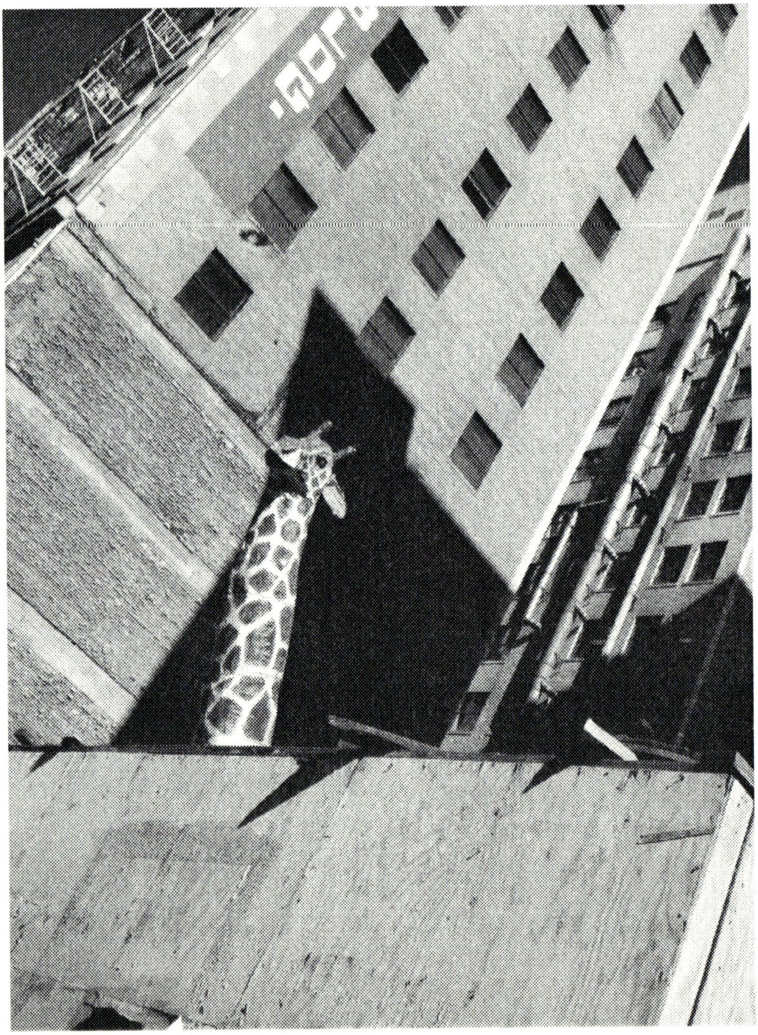

The Happiest Men in L.A.

The happiest men in L.A.
are in love with those women
who understand
that all men want is daily sex,
and after that, a sandwich.

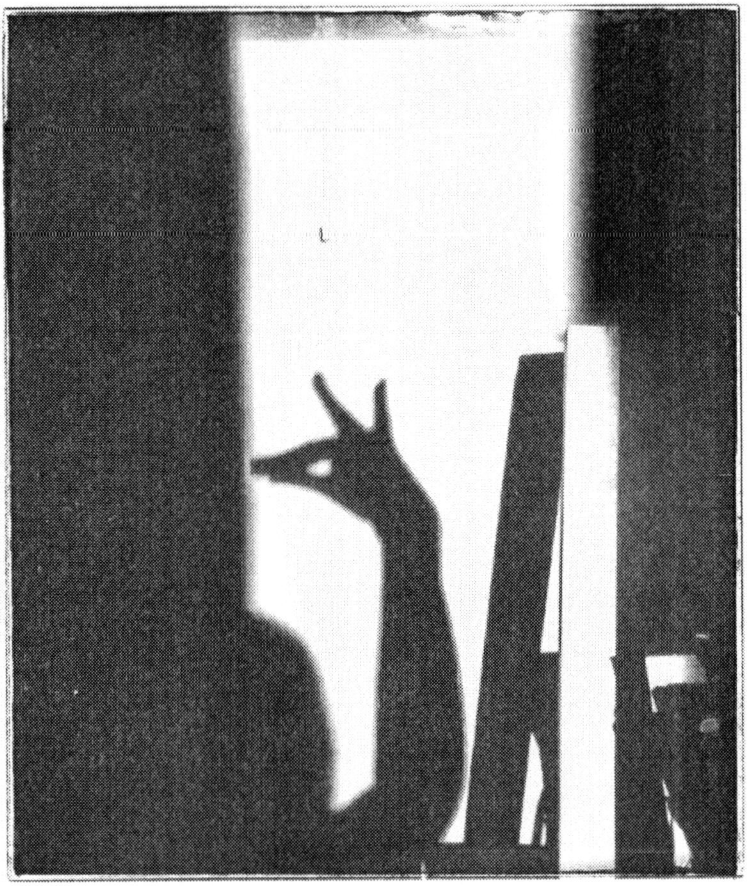

At Twelve, The Awakening

O! backyard see-saw,
days spent courting
steel between my legs,
the thrilling rub
that knew no name.

Forgive my mother,
turning from the window;

Forgive my father,
hi-ball in hand;

Forgive my uncle,
hiding in the juniper hedge
hand down his pants;

Forgive me my
furious pumping,

oblivious,

the curious damp
an addiction,

a glimpse of my future.

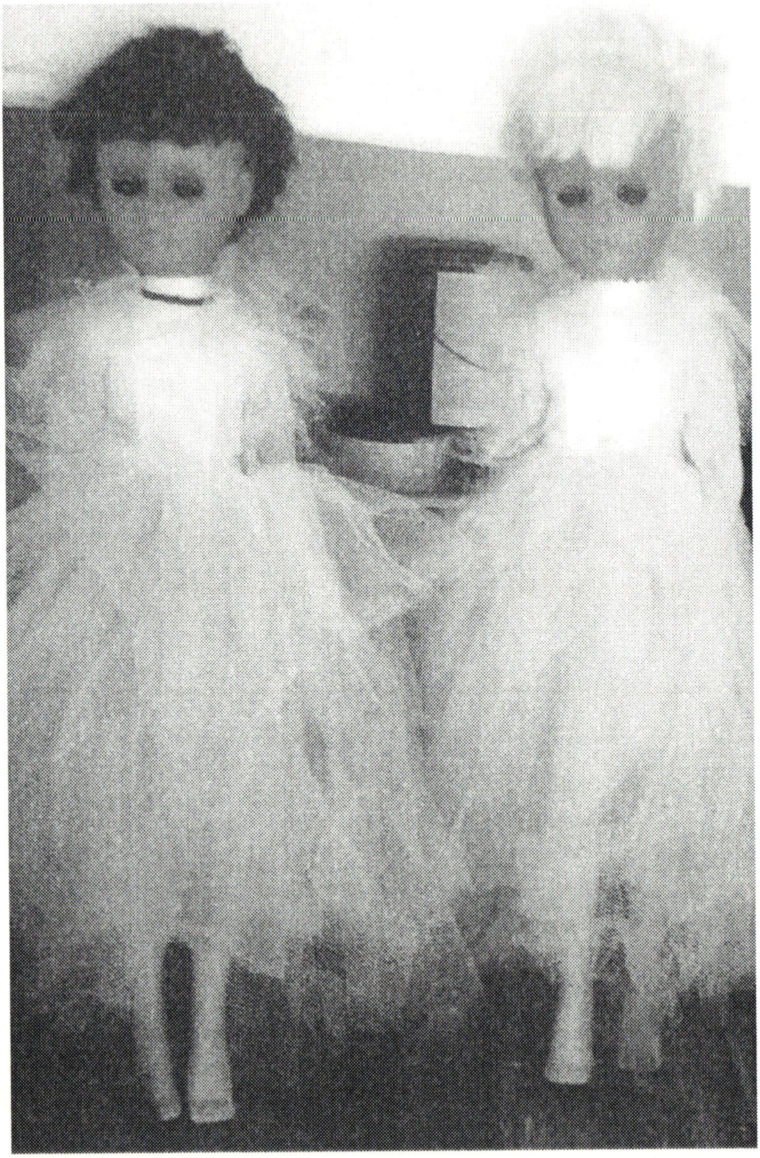

99-Seat Waver

I fell out of love with Bertolt
Brecht when we were cast in
that potboiler, "Drums In The
Night." You played
Whore #1. I played
Whore #2. You'd just
divorced your 3rd
husband for the 2nd time.
My starter husband
was fucking my best
friend while I rehearsed.
I was fucking no one until
you took a shine to me.
I'd forgotten how it felt
to be touched.

In the dressing room
you'd push me up
against the wall,
slip your hand
down my pants,
and diddle me silly.

When the director
caught us,
he said one word.

"Typecasting."

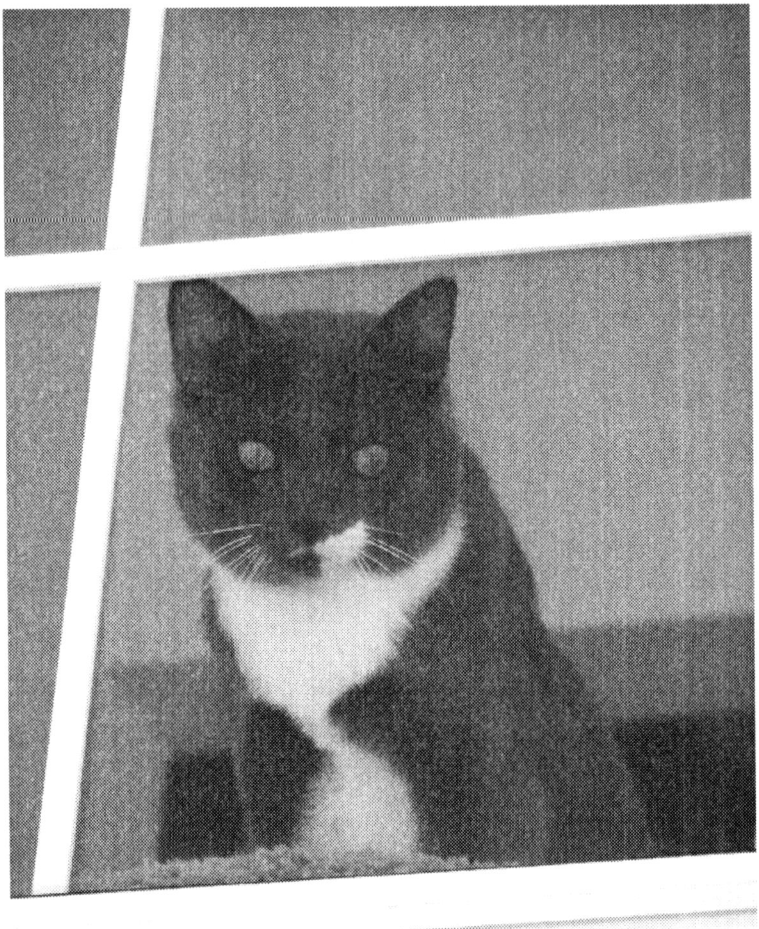

Territory

He flaunts my love bites on his lips,
my kisses hang on his
words. He takes me to parties,
to get me off. It's foreplay.
Our last assignation found us in
my ex-boyfriend's kitchen,
my ass flush with the
travertine countertops,
pencil skirt hiked above my thighs.
I like to keep
in touch with old friends.
He likes marking his territory.

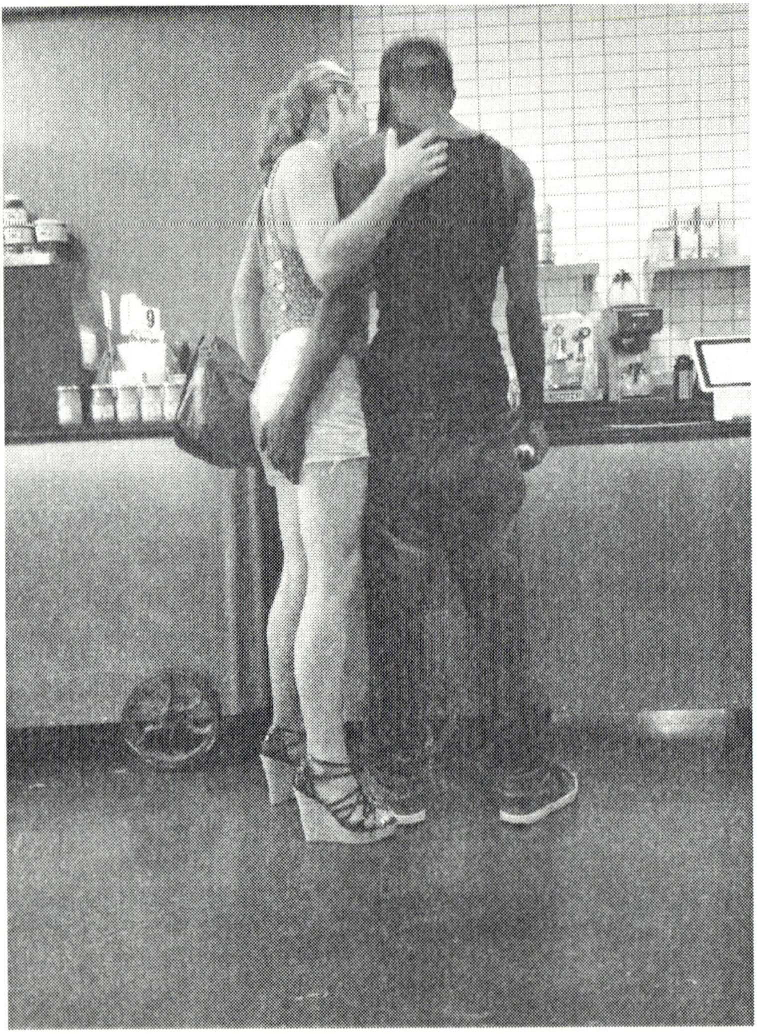

Your Target

The last man I fucked before my husband is
standing in the shampoo aisle at my local Target when
our carts collide. He's not surprised to see me.

"I knew I would find you here," he says in
that French accent I once found irresistible. "After all,
this is *your* Target." He pronounces it like it's some
high-end sex boutique instead of Walmart with
better commercials.

I spent three years in his bed. I brought the pussy.
He supplied the passion and the pot. He had the biggest
cock I'd seen, and if size had been the measure
of a relationship, we'd never have parted.

How do you tell your ex that he opened you up,
made you ripe for the one true love who followed?

The last man I fucked before my husband grabs my hand,
brings it to his lips. "I heard you were married?" he asks,
a flicker of hope in his eyes. I nod; he sighs.

"When I taught you how to love again," he says. "I thought
you would love me."

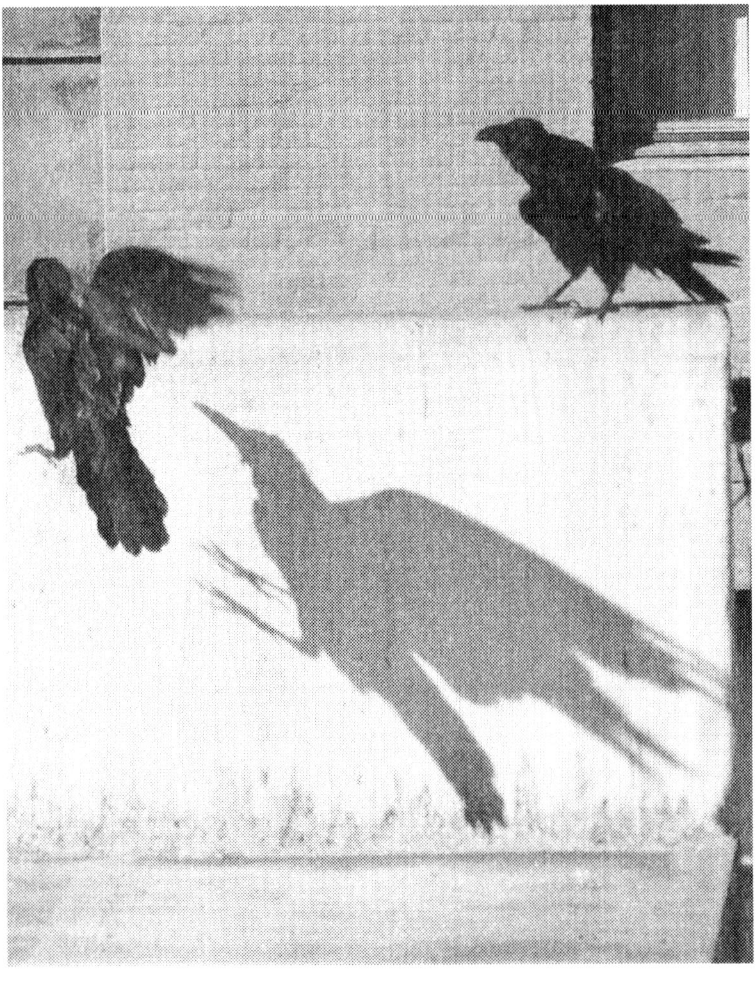

Upon Running into My Ex on a Summer Afternoon

1.
we up broke.
got back ack ack.
broke down, betty.
open,
broke open like eggs,
crack crack.
we had a rhythm,
a mad love,
mad, I tell you!

2.
how long's it been, baby?
you up still to
no good?

3.
oh, that hot
tequila night
I dressed in
moonbeams
still gets
under
your skin, huh?

4.
I know.
I know.
everybody lies.
everybody up fucks.
everybody.

5.
who still loves you, baby?
That's right.
That's right.
You got that right.
Nobody but me.

Flashbacks

I have flashbacks
of him and me in those count 'em on one hand times when
we were precisely in sync, and
we fucked like a well-oiled machine
drilling, filling,
spilling. oh

I have flashbacks
of him and me in those I'll never forget 'em moments when
we'd climax together
a single being
for a second. A blink.
When I felt safe.

I have flashbacks
of him and me surrendering... No. Me surrendering
him observing, packing it away for later when
he needed something on me, something
like my vulnerability. My perversions. My secret heart.

I have flashbacks
of him and me, see us naked, on the bed,
curved into one another, his body pressed into mine,
his penis already hard against my ass,
his long, black leanness, protective, like he has my back.

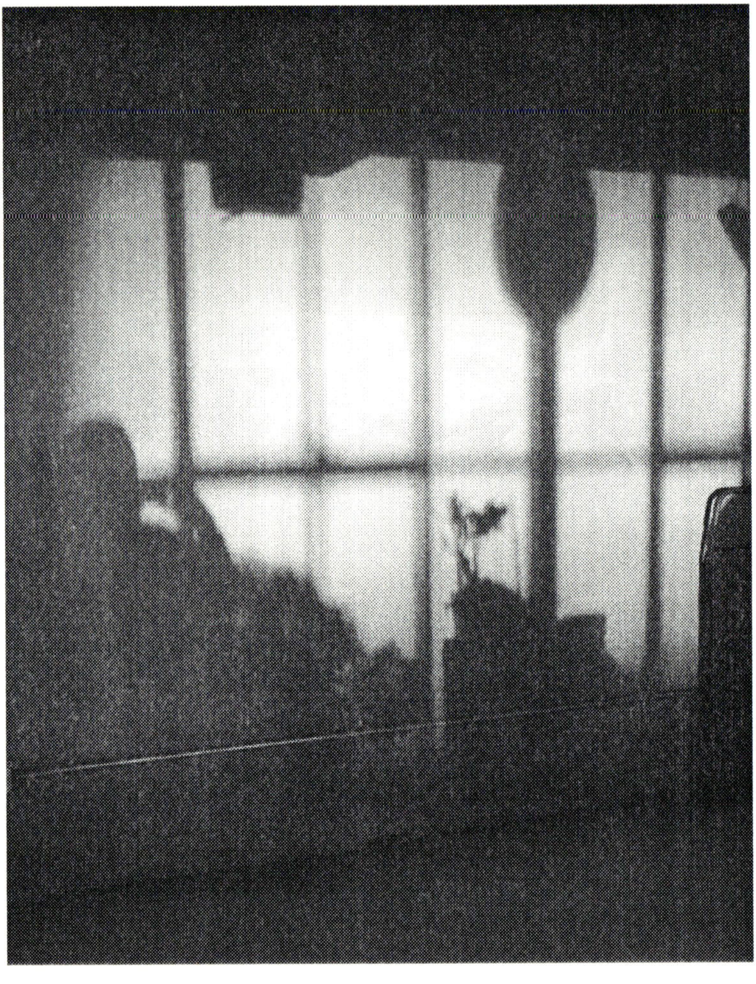

Mayonnaise

the lotion spurts out of the bottle like mayonnaise,
like your thick white cum shoots between my breasts & across
my face.
it's good for the complexion, you say.
I rub it in. lick the alabaster bitter from my
fingers.

never enough times will I lie with you here, ocean's cool wafting from
the half-cracked window,
Etta James crooning from those high-end
speakers, the air like
jasmine, and me, open mouthed, ready, today's blue plate
special, all smooth & creamy; calibrated for your dining
pleasure.
A toast, my precious darling: I give you mine.
you give me yours. mingled.
melded into mmmmmmmmmmm.
our penis, our balls, our succulent breasts, our absolutely famished
vagina.

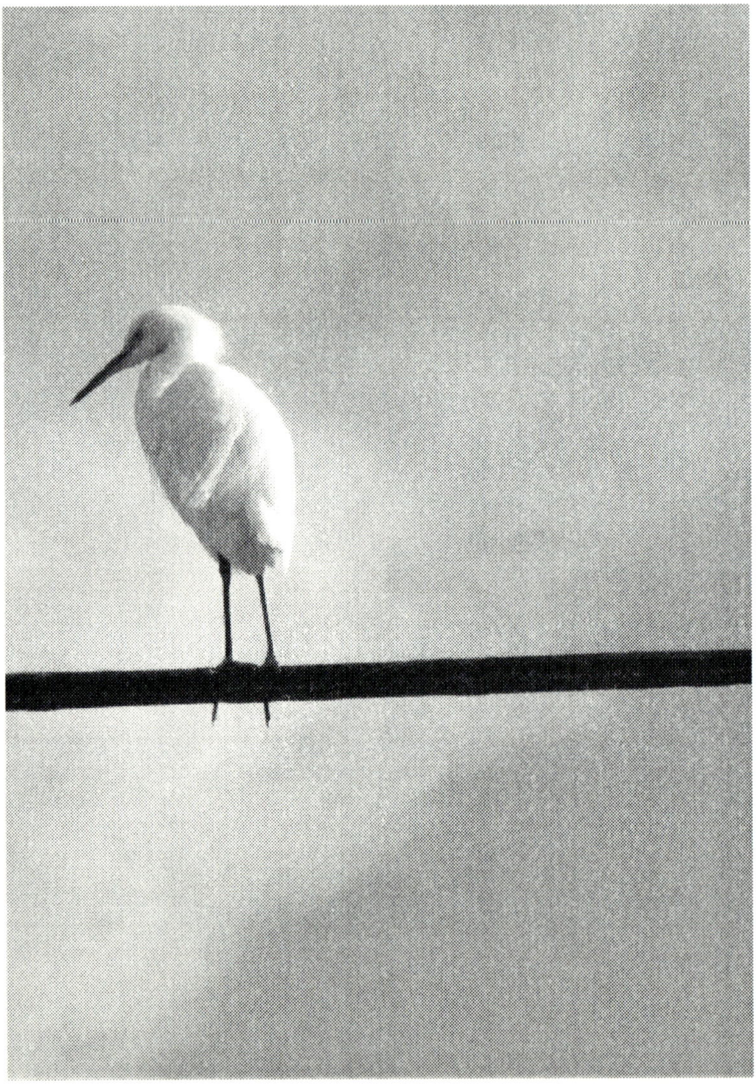

Allison L.

She has a mole
on her
lower back.
I'd glimpse it
when she'd
bend over
or squat down.
She has agile knees.
Great tits.
A perfect piece of ass.

When I saw the mole
it was exciting,
a dark secret,
a sneak peek at
Nirvana;
it made me wet,
& I'd kiss it
with my eyes.

When we were
together
I did more
than that.
Lots more.

She told me she
liked it.
Till she didn't.
Till she left me.
Till she kicked me to
the curb.

Her small, black
imperfection
blends into night,
swallows her up;
a rodent is how
I imagine her
now.
A mole.
Night-eyes.
Night-eyes.

O! Allison,
Tell me why?
I am left
in the dark
&
I'm looking, but
I can't find
all my pieces.

Under Water

Forget them. The men who looked right through you, used you up,
the ones you opened wide for when you should have run.
Forget about pop songs you listened to in secret, ones that made you
think someone was out there, just for you. It isn't true.
Forget the fumblers, the degenerates,
the bad boys, the all-that-you deserves.
That fast-talking charmer who popped your cherry in the dark?
The baller who refused to give you head? The rich kid
who left you at the hotel, holding the bill? All bastards, still.
Don't line up all those New Year's Eves
when everyone else was a couple.
That line will conga out the door. Nothing comes easy.
Nothing goes right.
You swear it builds character, or some Nietzsche shit.
You don't sleep at night.
You deserve to rut in those desperate times,
daddy's bourbon in your glass,
mama's Vicodin in your pocket, those B-movie plots in your head.
Given the choice,
you'll always go with the angrier option, the one that guarantees pain.
Admit it!
You're a sucker for drama. It's tattooed across your forehead,
neon-lit behind your eyes.
You've gone over it a million times and still you're none the wiser.
So do yourself a favor. Forget trust. Forget love.
Forget your goddam dreams.
Forget your happy childhood, the ponies, the neglect.
Forget your straight A's, your perfect pitch,
your mastery of all things French.
Forget about having a normal life; it's all rubbed out, erased,
because you can't forget the pool man
who grabbed you in the deep end,
who stripped you, squeezed you till you cried, till you let him touch you,
till you let him finger you, till you admitted it felt good.

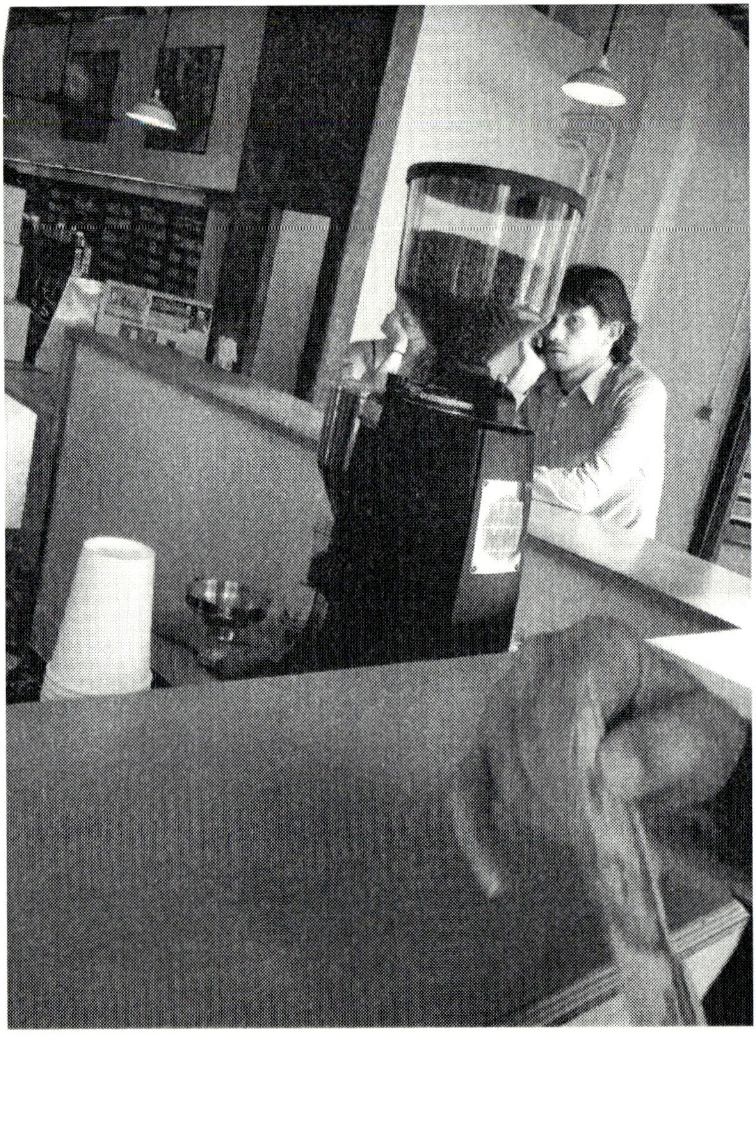

White Flag
On Edward Hopper's painting, "Morning Sun," 1952

No one paints loneliness like he does. Those half-clad women by the bed, on the floor, hunched over, staring out the window, in profile or from behind, always clean lines, such worshipful light. The gas station in the middle of nowhere, estranged couples on the bright-lit porch after dark. Even the boats sail alone. And the diners. The hatted strangers, coming on to a redhead, a moody blonde, all of them losers, all of them desperate for a second chance. This morning the sunlight pried open my eyes, flooded our bedroom walls. I sat alone, in profile on our bed in a pink chemise, knees drawn up, arms crossed over my calves, staring out the window. Desperate for you. No one paints loneliness like Edward Hopper paints me, missing you, apologies on my lips. Come back. Stand below my window. Watch me beg for a second chance. Downturned mouth, sad eyes, parted knees, open thighs, that famous shaft of Hopper light a white flag, if only you could see.

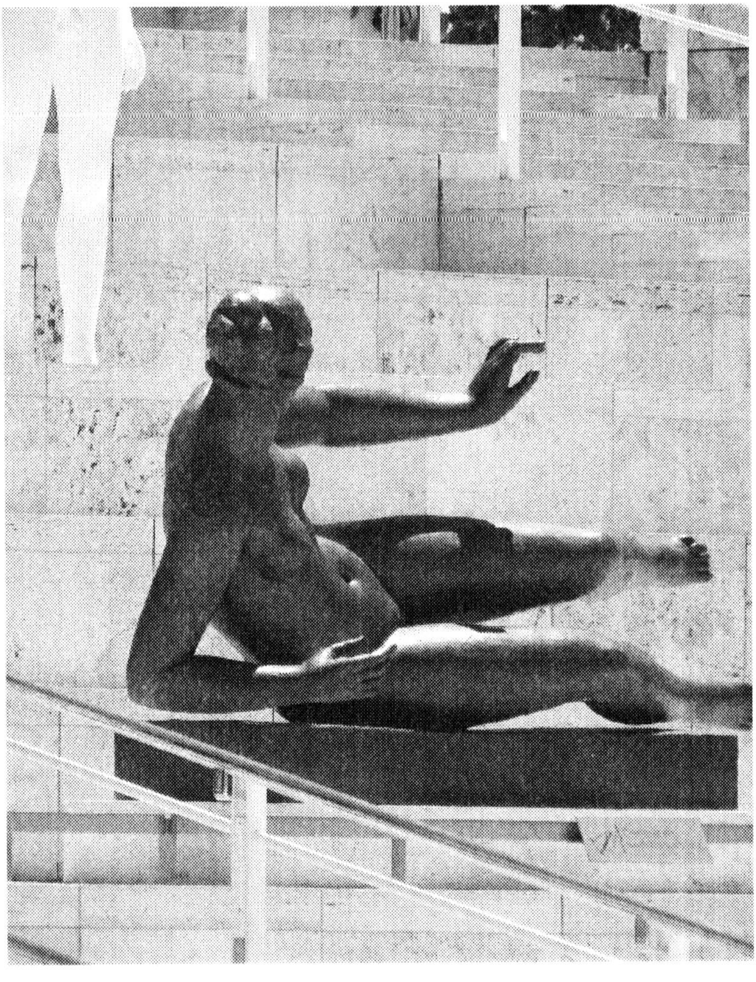

Staying Put
after Edward Hopper's painting, A Woman In The Sun, 1961

He paints me naked in an empty room.
Like I need nothing. Like he needs me.
I'm his type.
High tits. Lean shadow,
blond hair falling
past my shoulders.
A long drink of water.

There is no escape.
But the window to my left is a promise.
Wide open. Green hills, ripe with longing.
"Hold still!" he says.

So I stare at the painting on the wall.
Another landscape, this one contained
by a white mat, black frame,
it, too, allows for dreaming. But it only
goes so far, then hits the wall. Like him.
Only so far before he drops off-grid and
disappears into the canvas. No
wonder I can't stay still.

The room holds little. A bed, my shoes
abandoned underneath. A pack of
cigarettes. My restless heart. A rectangular shaft
of light pours in from an open, second window and
the breeze plays with my hair.
"Fix it!" he says.

I tuck the wisp of hair behind my right ear,
just the way he likes it, then put my hand
back where it belongs.

He says his favorite thing is painting sunlight
on the side of a house.
"So why paint me all the time?" I ask.
"So you'll stay put."

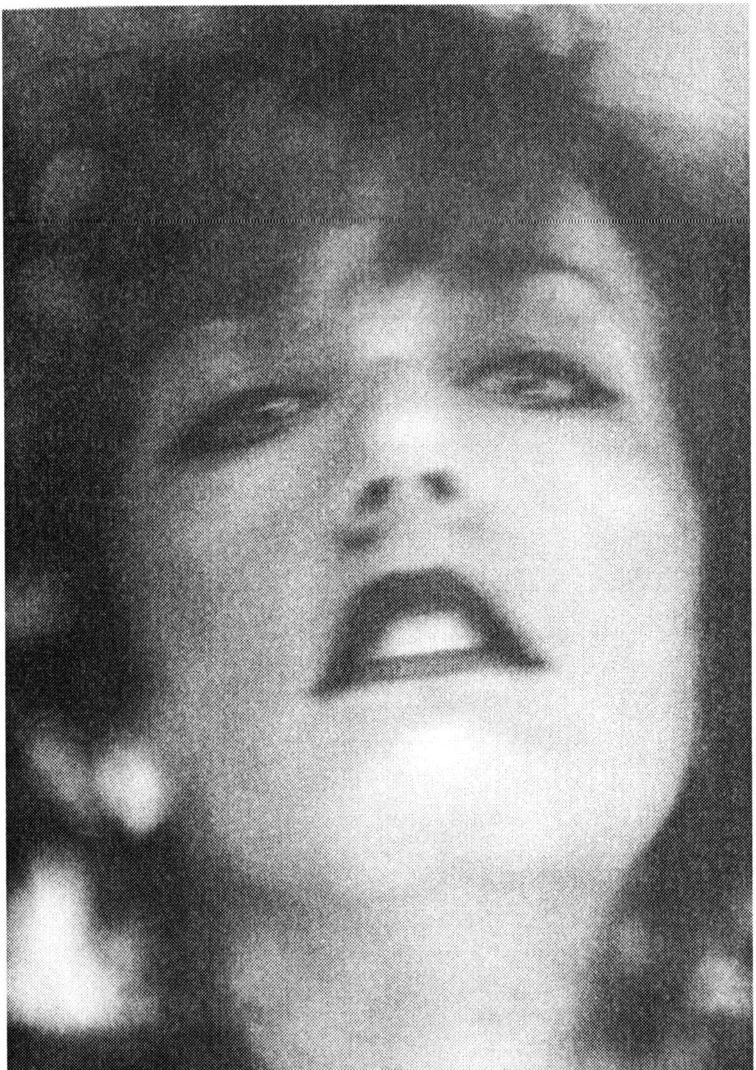

When Two Poets Collide: For Anna After the Most Recent Breakup
after a photo by Philip-Lorca diCorcia

Anna Andreyevna is at the bar,
resplendent in a white dress that
rides her thighs, cups her lying, Ruskie
ass. She wears it to torture
me. Ditto those killer red stilettos.

Still, the slant of her leg, wedged just
below the bar, is unforgettable.

The barkeep flicks on the overheads.
Everything looks better.
Neon makes Anna look trustworthy.
I can't look away.

Her favorite bar. *Her* part of town.
Someone whispers in
my ear. "Go home!
She will never leave with you."
But I stay to watch Anna
dance with the other losers.

It is always the same.
We drink too much vodka.
It gets late. I wait. I am only human.

Finally Anna dances with me,
shoves her sweaty breasts at me,
her white ass firm in my hands. She
reaches between my legs,
grabs it like she owns me.
"Is this what you want?" she asks,
eyes blazing.

She's tipsy,
but I have no shame.
Tomorrow, she will hate me,
but tonight?
We will fuck as poets fuck.

Like Sisyphus At the Chateau Marmont

I'd slip out of my skirt, my thong,
(*my attitude*),

pull the sweater
over my head.

Arrange my body
on the bed.

I'd go wet at the thought of you.
It washed me clean
and stupid.

Down on all fours like a fucking dog,
doing what my mama warned me
not to do, throwing good
money after bad.

Did I mention how much I liked it?

We had a history,
all dead ends.

You brought the handcuffs
I'd make amends.

We already know exactly
how it ends.

You lie. I believe.
I submit, you deceive.

My body turns to you like a dahlia
seeks the sun

and then you run.

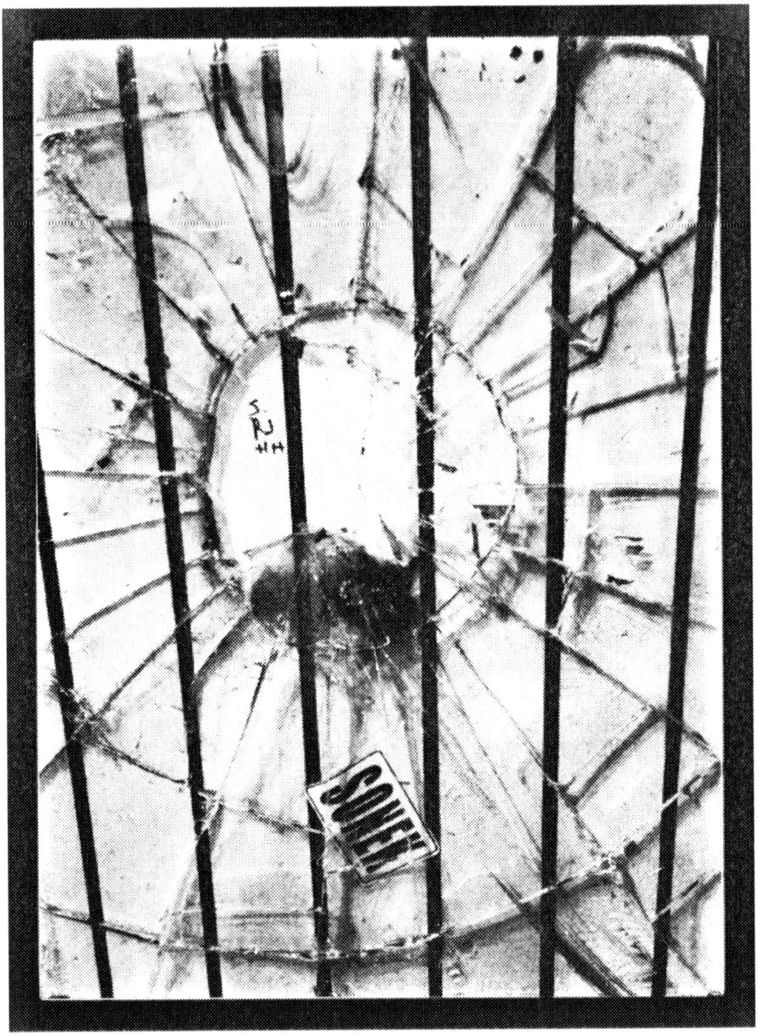

Rape Reality

not the feather bed.
handcuffs
edged in lace.

back alley.
punch in the face.

not the slow tease.
soft caress.
perfect teeth.
fragrant breath.

swoop and grab
street slab gritty
where the dogs piss.

throws her down.

bludgeons.

not a coax. no
sweet surrender,

repeat offender.

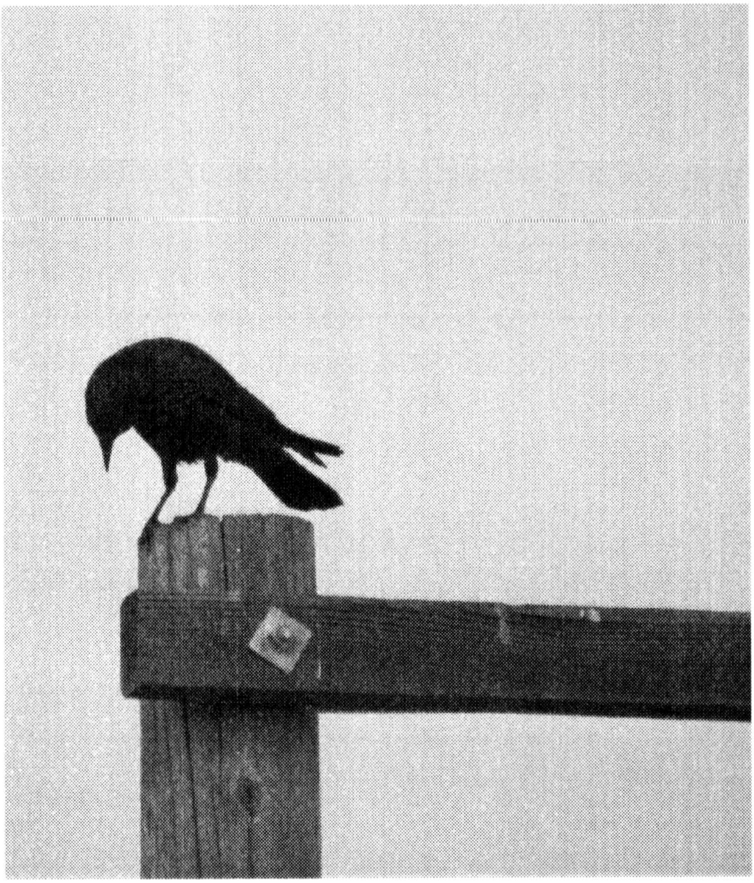

When

The regret that hides out inside our eyes when we say goodbye
when we see each other one last time when we wish we'd never
laid eyes on each other when we know for certain we've fallen
out of love when we realize we've made a mistake when he
back-pedals apologies and I grab his hand out of habit

and there's that fucking spark

and then there's him, pulling me in
when I'm fragile and he has the upper hand
when he sticks his tongue down my throat
when I get that swirly feeling in my cunt

when I want him to stop when I don't want him to stop
when he slips his hand inside my jeans when he wedges his
thumb inside my panties when I ache for the thrust of him

when he pushes me onto the bed when he takes my breasts in his hands
when his tongue moves down my body when I admit
he knows best how I like it when he admits he can't live without me

The regret that hides out inside my body
when my husband gets back in town.

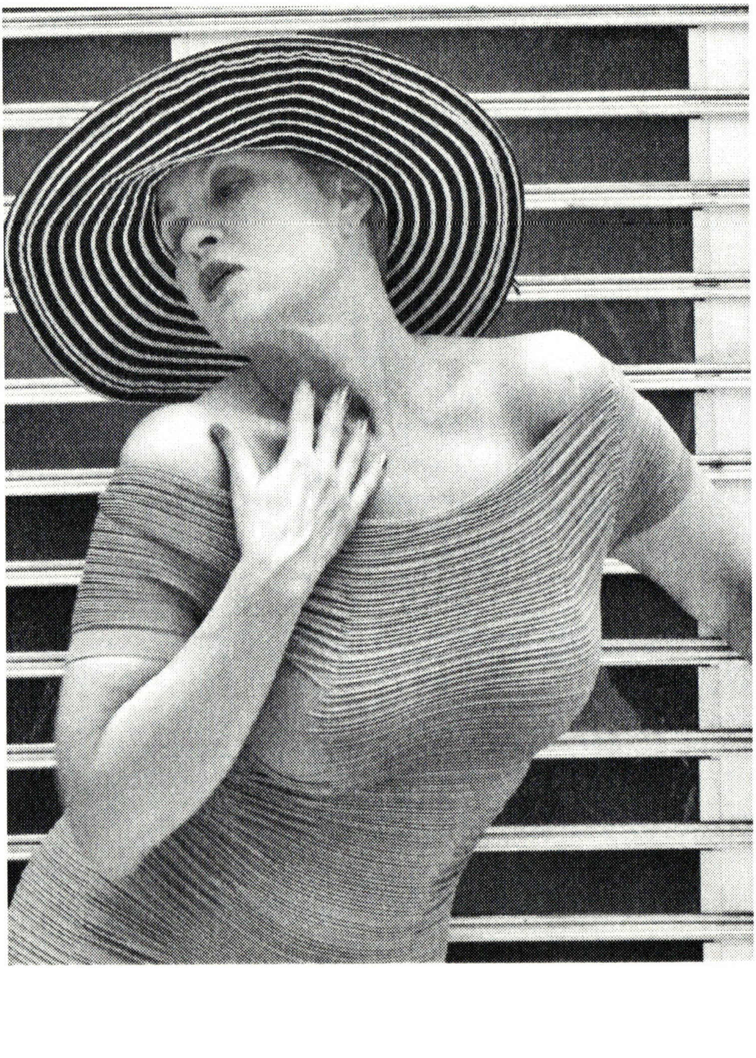

The Narcissist's Confession

Before I was your wife I
was a narcissist.
Before that, I was a dyke.

Before you, I loved an artist. Big
cock. No ambition. I wanted him
to change. His cock shrank.

I poured sugar in his gas tank
to teach him a lesson.

What civilized person
acts like that?

Before I was your wife I loved a
woman. After sex,
her scent lingered
on my upper lip.
Eau de Desperation.

But you, baby,
smell like success, old,
east-coast money,
Episcopalian bebop, those
blue eyes focused Godward when
you come.

It took me forever,
stepping on them to get to
you. Sometimes
I wonder how
I managed to climb
over all those
bodies.

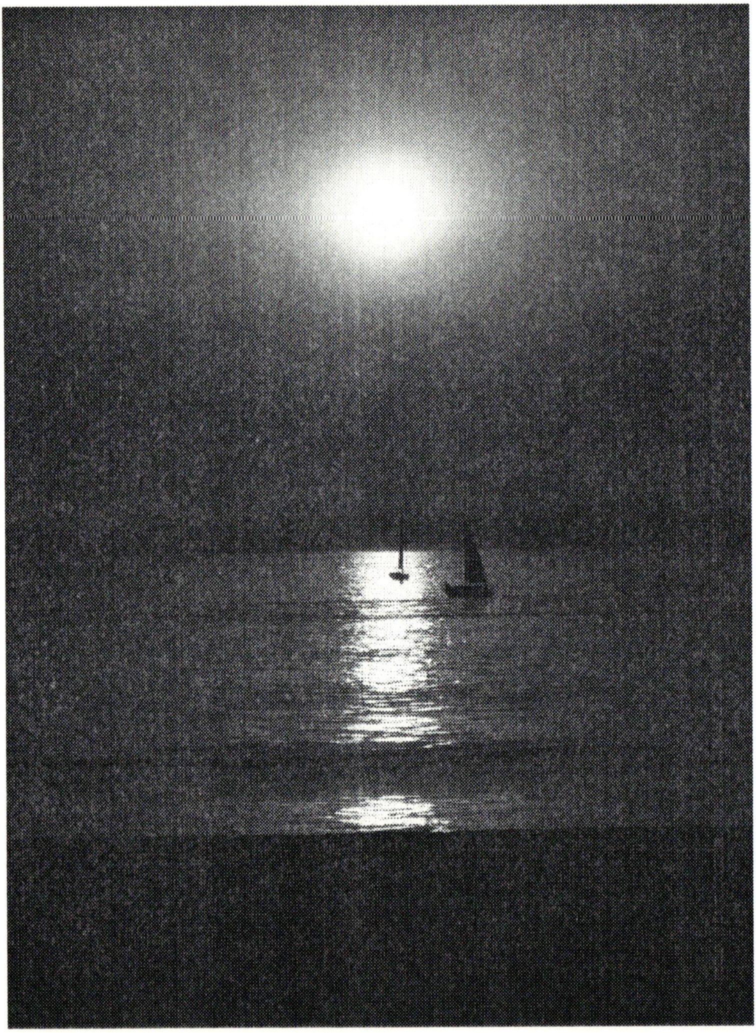

Dos Gardenias
for K o'D

I need to tell you how days drag now
that you're gone; no phone calls or Skype.

The light is never bright or warm. No one
wants to dance. Today I emptied an old bottle

of your pills, packed it with Hindu Kush,
drove to the beach. Lit up.

It's legal now in California.

I play your favorite music; Buena Vista
Social Club, Ibrahim Ferrer.

Remember that yellow bikini you used to wear?
It made you look invincible, like a star.

I'd wear the Che Guevara cap you brought
from Cuba when we danced, girl on girl
to *Dos Gardenias*. Our song.

Your breasts crushing mine.
Those signature gardenias pinned in your hair.

Now I dance alone, my screen dark.
I will not weep. You'd hate it.

Since you died, I play *Dos Gardenias*
every day, and the way the palm trees sway
breaks my heart.

You're out there, dancing,
aren't you?

Your yellow bikini a beacon, if only I could find it
in the star-crossed night.

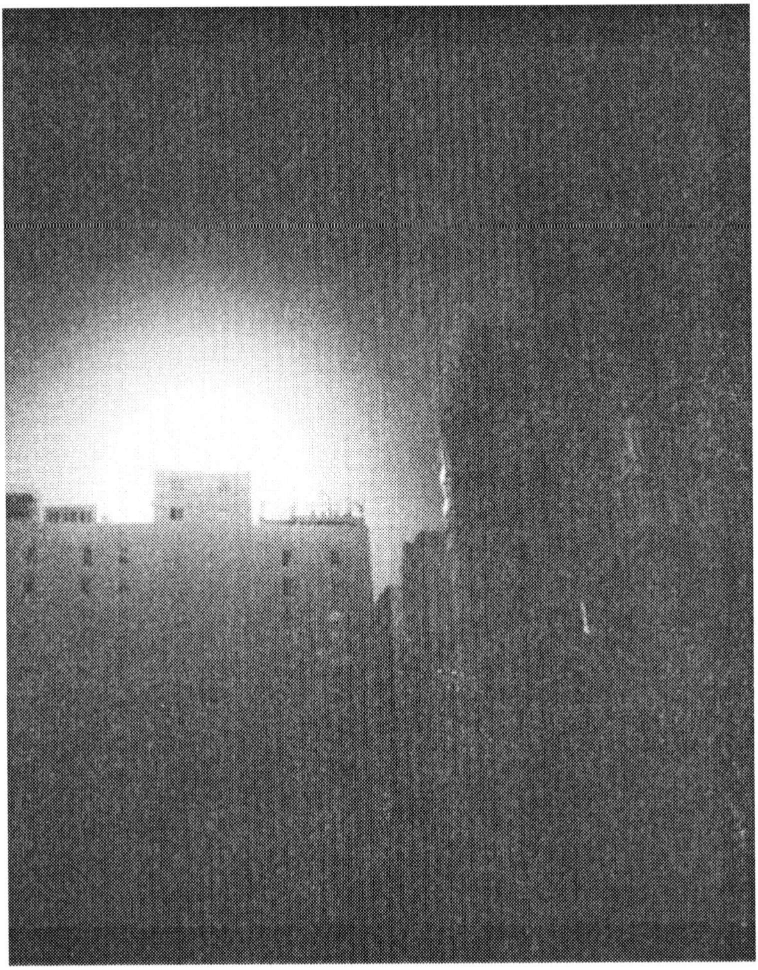

At Last! Blues for Etta James

Hers was the voice of an angel, a total access backstage pass for her skin-tight sheath, platinum wig, that honey-dripping skin. Oh! *It Must Be Love!* & it was, in all its tattered colors that found her yielding to the drum, the bass, the piano man, the sweeping violins, that tempted her to fall into that needy place of more depth, more soul, more inspiration. (I mean when you start out that good, where you gonna go from there?)

Oh, baby, remember the night of the thousand Cosmopolitans? When we walked the Speedway Alley between Mast St. & Venice Blvd.? It was Happy Hour at the Canal Club. We slurped buck-a-piece oysters & ate California rolls & danced to Etta James on the jukebox, tossing back those $5, whatever's in the well vodka Cosmos. Etta was singing *"A Sunday Kind of Love,"* & I was safe in your arms.

Hers was a dark pursuit. *"I'd rather go blind,"* she sang, *"than to see you walk away from me."* Her story. Or her mama's, giving birth all alone at 14. Swore her daddy was Minnesota Fats. Or that's the skinny. A West Coast, church-singing foster girl. Inconvenient. Never loved enough girl. Poor Jamesetta! They turned her name around but not her life.

Oh It Must Be Love! & it was, baby, you & me in the clutch of us, glued, skin on skin, oh it must be love! Grinding past the dance floor, into the street, illumined by neon, by starlight & moon, you dry humped me in the alley, all the while, that Etta crooned, *"Roll With Me, Henry!"* Too down & dirty for the radio. *Gotta roll, all night long...*

& the saxophone growled heroin, the guitar screeched cocaine. Ms. Etta didn't know enuf to come in from the rain. Didn't know enuf to guard her open heart, didn't even know to put the horse before the cart.

That would have been a good thing, baby. A cart to take us home, a cab to hail. Instead, we walked back alone, sloppy drunk, we wove our way down Speedway in the midnight hour, singing Etta's theme song *a cappella*. A light rain came out of nowhere. The moon lit our way home. "I love you, baby," you whispered, your lips lost in my hair. *"At Last!"* I said, & wondered if Etta had ever felt such love, ever known such bliss, ever heard those words from someone who really meant them.

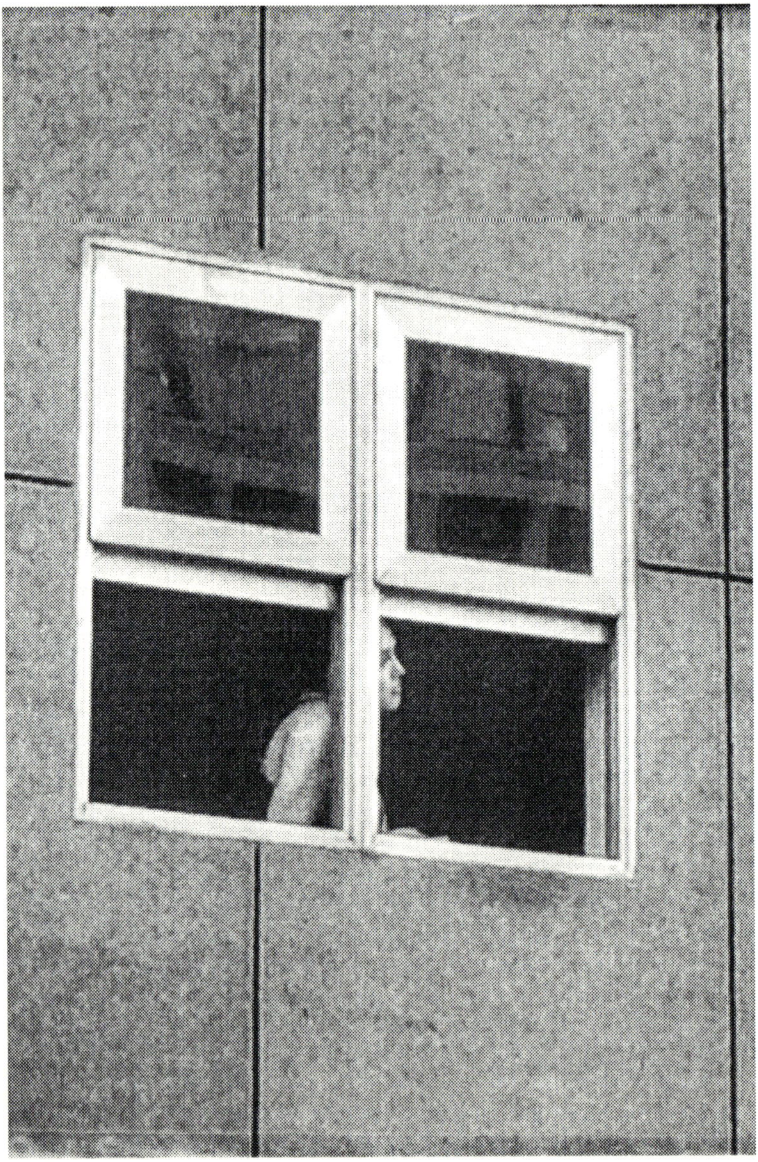

Blackberry Haiku

it was a hot day.
I ate the cold blackberries.
you slept through it all.

I was hung over.
just a minor case of spins.
it fucked up my day.

you went bike riding.
then you came back here to sleep.
the berries beckoned.

I was so inspired
that I stayed behind & wrote
hungover writing.

I'd suck you off if
you were wide awake right now
instead of sleeping.

I eat while you sleep.
Crime of opportunity.
I'd do it again.

I confess, okay?
I ate all the blackberries
& then you woke up.

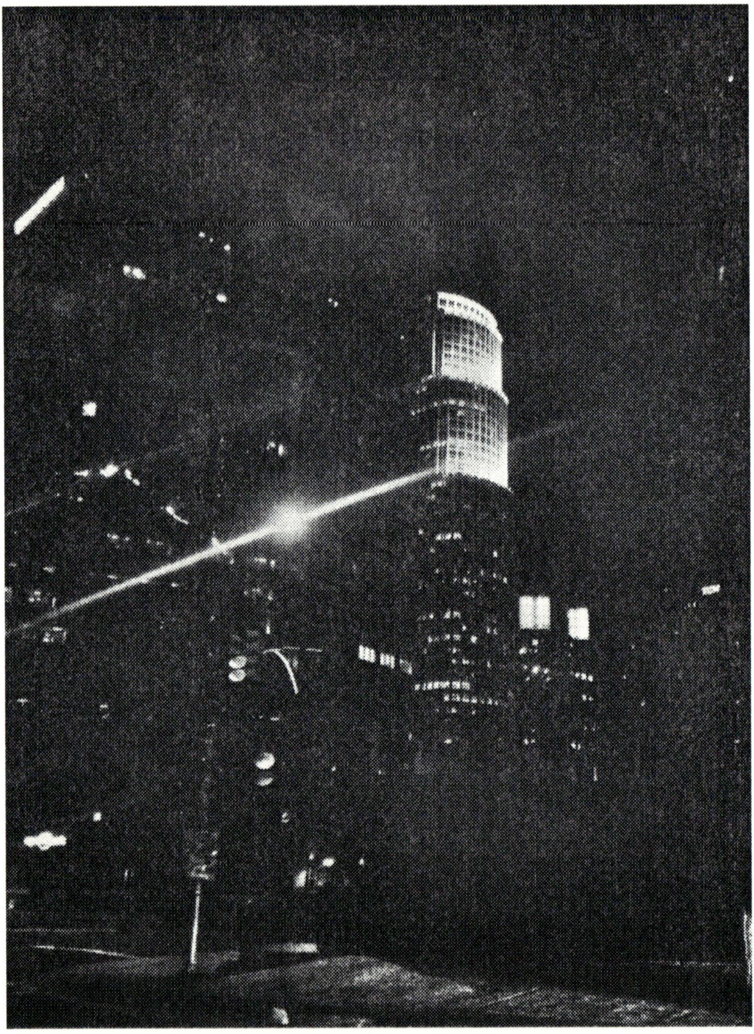

Walk All Over You

The stiletto boots in the back of my closet are
restless, long to stroll the 3rd Street Promenade,
looking for a red silk bustier. A Louis Vuitton bag.
A lover who won't let me down.

The stiletto boots in the back of my closet
want to party, want to grab my feet,
climb my calves, hug my thighs. They're
ready for action. Ready to put on a skintight
Versace, and head for the club.

They want to clack on terrazzo floors,
totter from great heights, see the world.
Escape the flats, the Mary Jane's, the penny
loafers, the two-toned, two-faced saddle Oxfords
that guard the closet door.

The stiletto boots in the back of my closet
want to walk all over you, punish you for
cheating, make you pay.
They have a short memory, don't care
why they were banished or what you
did. They're desperate to reclaim you,
dig their heels into your shortcomings,
make little marks up and down your libido.
Welcome you home.

They long to wrap themselves around
you, put you in a headlock, rake your thighs,
want to lead you into ecstasy.
Saran Wrap.
Whipped cream.
Wesson Oil.
Room service.
Remember?

My stilettos can't forget you.
My stilettos can't move on.
My stilettos want to forgive you.
Even if I cannot.

They bear the scuff marks
of your betrayal far better than do I.

The stiletto boots in the back of my closet
are negotiating their release, want me
to give you a second chance
to trample my heart.

Like the last time and the time before.
They want to get started, head out the door.
Who do you think gave me those fucking boots,
anyway?

La Petite Mort

A little death,
that moment of
falling,
like holding
your breath
till stars appear

in
free-fall you
spend it all -
the spilling -
what you most desire,
on fire for a few
seconds.

While you pray to
the Lazarus
inside
for yet another
day,
another ride,

your seed pouring
down
my
thigh

another little death
or a million.

Don't be afraid to dream a little bigger, darling.

College Roomates

I asked for it, coming
home 2 am, disheveled,
reeking sex. Every
weekend for a year.

It was my fault,
always in his face,
those skimpy clothes,
teasing him with
my inaccessibility.
I knew he knew I was
giving it away.

I wasn't surprised when
he sat in wait, pushed me
up against the dresser,
grabbed my breasts,
tore at my blouse,
ripped my skirt, shoved
himself into me, even
then, only half-hard.

I didn't mind the rape.
It was the softness I minded,
how he couldn't get it up
when it mattered.
I fell for hard men
with bad intentions.
Not men who loved me.

We never spoke of it
but his shame hung in the air,
that hangdog apology
in his eyes, the
unrequited love that
spoiled him for
anyone else.

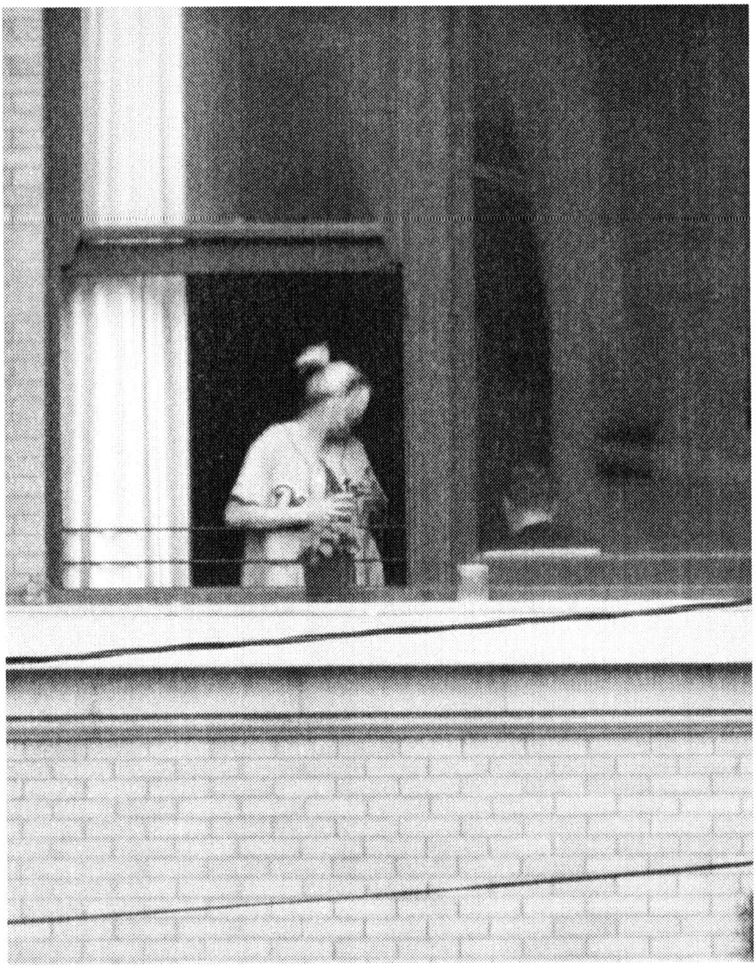

Nebraska

"We never talk," he said. "If my dick got soft, you wouldn't even know me." He gathered his clothes off the floor. His defection took me by surprise. "I feel like a stud horse," he muttered. Like that was a bad thing. That last night we lay spooned in what I thought was the afterglow. For the first time since I'd left for college, I felt my life was together. He looked like Robert Redford, his body farmhand hard, already leathered; he smelled like sunlight on the plains. I called him "Nebraska," and when I thought of him, I pictured him with a blade of straw between his teeth the *exact* color of his hair. We'd meet Wednesdays and Saturdays, screw our brains out. Sometimes I'd even cook him dinner.

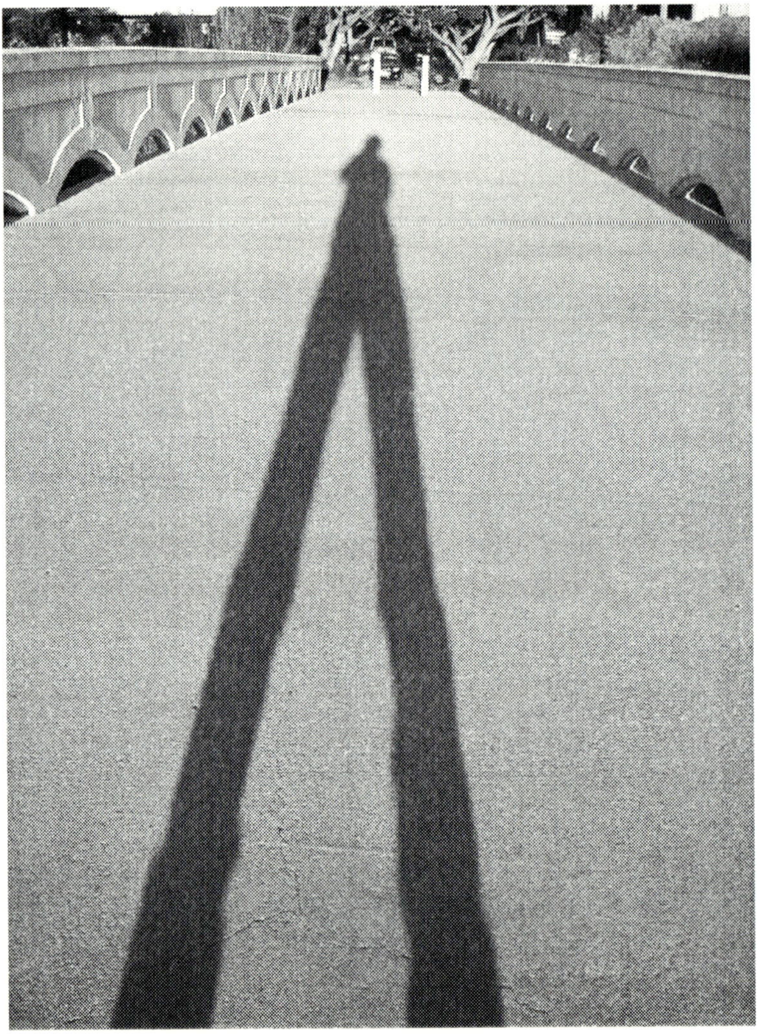

Dark Options

When you smile in your sleep I get nervous.
I know what you're capable of.
I've got the souvenirs to prove it, the fractured wrist
that never healed, the flinch when you
reach for my face.
I've learned to do what you tell me.
Make myself small.
Shut the fuck up.

Yesterday at the market I bought star fruit, endive, hollow points
and a pair of balls.
Thought I'd give the salad a little kick.

Sandmen have made themselves at home in your lashes.
Dark blood is matted in your hair.
It's 2 a.m. but I'm awake.
I could have shaved my legs, could have blown you when you
asked, stopped being (what did you call me?) a withholding bitch.

I like you best comatose, compromised, your back to me.
Red is your color.

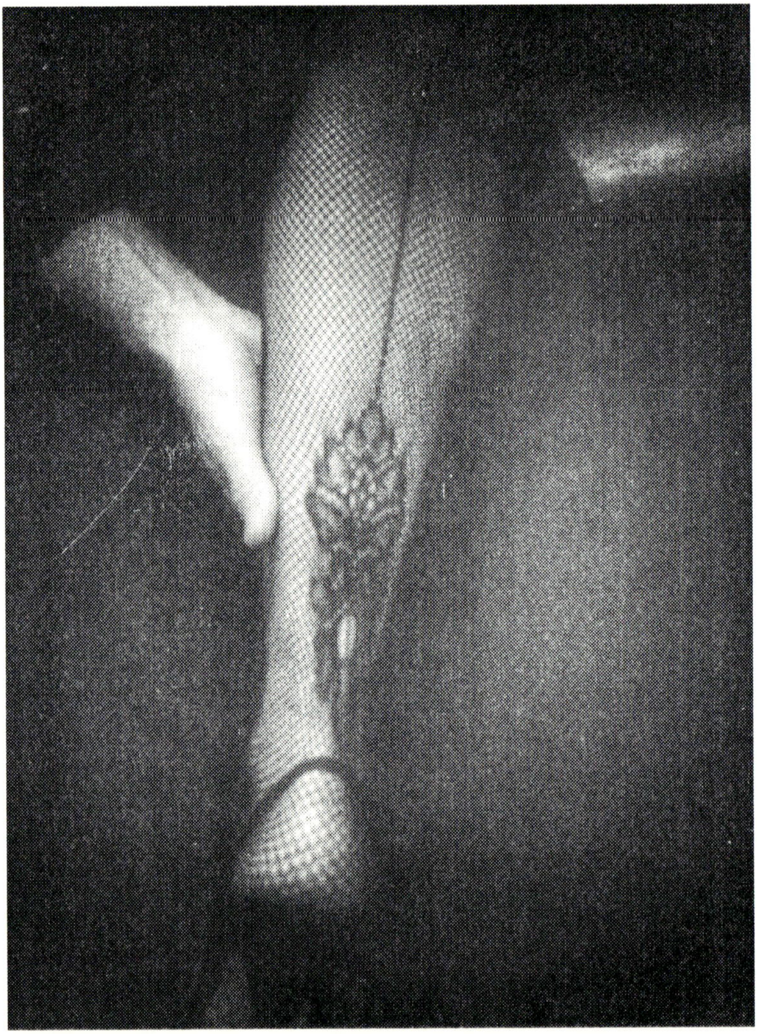

Pick Up - A 100-Word Story

Not Tiny's usual, lipstick lesbos, trannies. But tonight she wants to look up the skirt of the sad girl at the bar, buy her a Cosmopolitan. Follow her home. Sad girl toasts her latest benefactress, a charm bracelet rattling on her arm. "New Beginnings," she says, though she doesn't believe it. If new beginnings were gold charms she'd be rich, the bracelet too heavy for her slender wrist. No longer somebody's whore. Tiny catches a glimpse of the covered up bruise, the long scar right above her knee. The sad girl crosses her legs. A wall goes up. Like China.

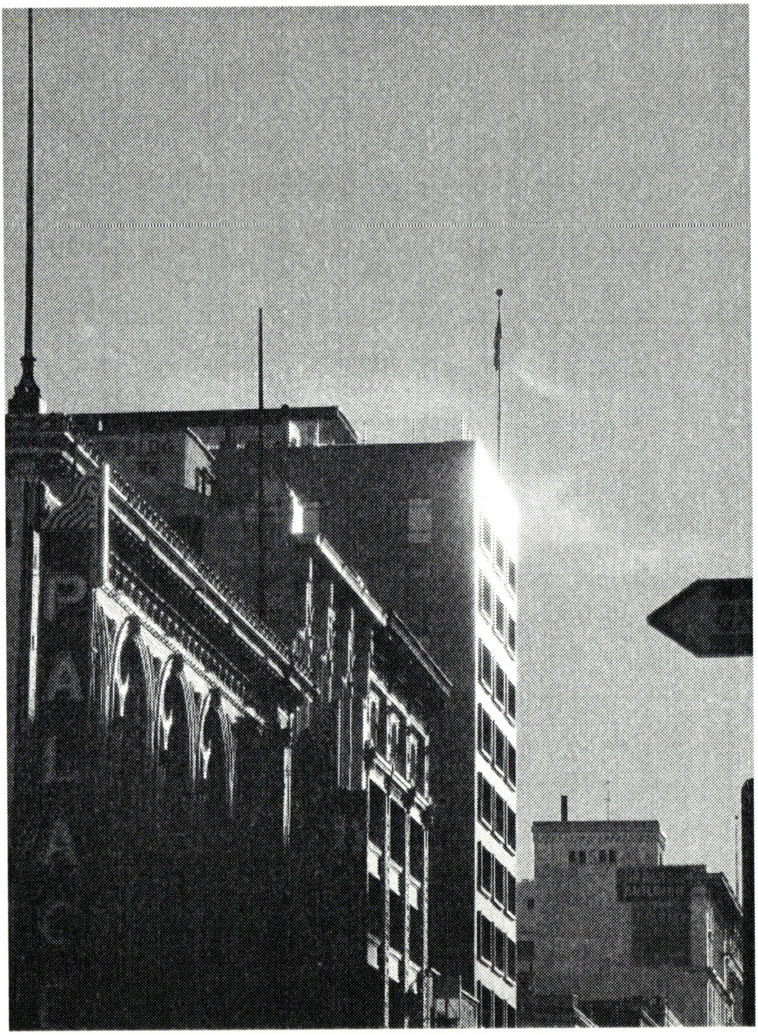

Something I Want to Tell You

back of you spooned
into me, ass moored
in
my belly's
harbor, your cock
swells
beneath my fingers.

you are almost
erect, and
find it hard to
pay attention.

but there's something I want to
tell you, how
this love broke me open,
my caution spilling
out of me like
your semen when
I rise from
our bed.

This love
has become me.

I could no more live
without you
than
breathe under water
or hang from my heels
on a star.

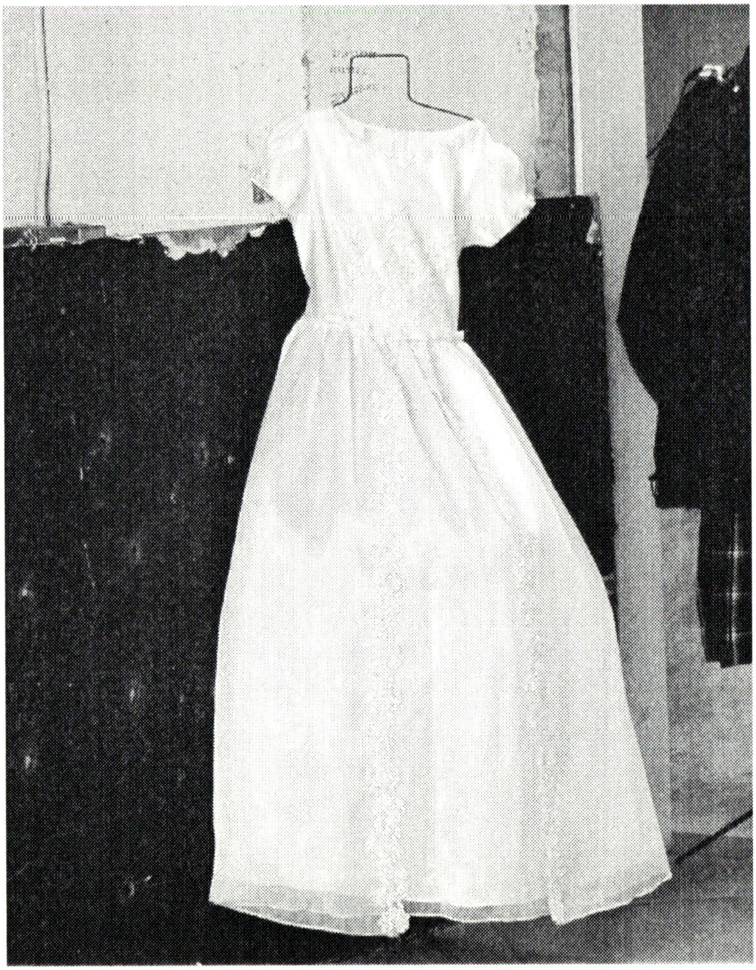

Second Chances

Remember those days in Chatsworth,
before all the porno stars moved in?
We made our own movies.

You'd grab my hips,
push up my dress, whisper obscenities
into my belly, your hot breath
a short cut to nirvana.

I keep thinking about your tongue,
how it could curl up,
twist from side to side,
make a girl very happy.

The last time we met I wore that
Donna Karan sheath you
bought me, the one with the
slit up the side.

It made me look so hot
you swore you wanted to
marry me.

Instead, we took risks. Shot drugs.
Let ourselves be seduced
by strangers.

I've been trying to get back
to you for years.

I keep thinking about your thumbs,
how they arch backward in
double-jointed ecstasy, perfectly
shaped for my clitoral pleasure.

The dress still fits.
I could wear it when you fuck me.
When we move back to Chatsworth,
we'll pretend we never left.

White People's Problems

the last time I saw Sally
she was on the wagon since
the night before,
said she didn't mind if I
had a drink, but burst
into tears and bolted at the
waiter's mere inquiry of "Stoli,
Grey Goose, Kettle One, or Sky?"

Sally and spouse had just restored
a million dollar hail Mary. just
finished the remodel and the pool.

how many times
can you not come home,
pass out cold, or
stumble, face down in
the pool, before one of
them notices?

Sally fucked the electrician
from Ecuador, twice.
both of them skunk drunk.
then they took a swim.

the sexless husband.
the self-absorbed spawn.
the soul-killing boredom.
certainly not how she pictured it.

when the parade marched
by my window, I grabbed
my camera, and began to shoot.
Ecuadorians lined the streets,
short and glowing, eager to show
their past, their new beginnings,
their American Dream.

the photo I didn't take
is of Sally, fucking her way
into oblivion while
parading Ecuadorians
build her house.

All the Rumors are True

I smell like your bed.
Not that I mind walking
bow-legged. I love
sex and especially with
you. It's not an imposition
the way it is for most
women, like they're doing
a man a favor. Each morning
you wake me with your
quotidian need. It feels like an
earthquake, only it goes on
longer. Then you periscope
towards me.

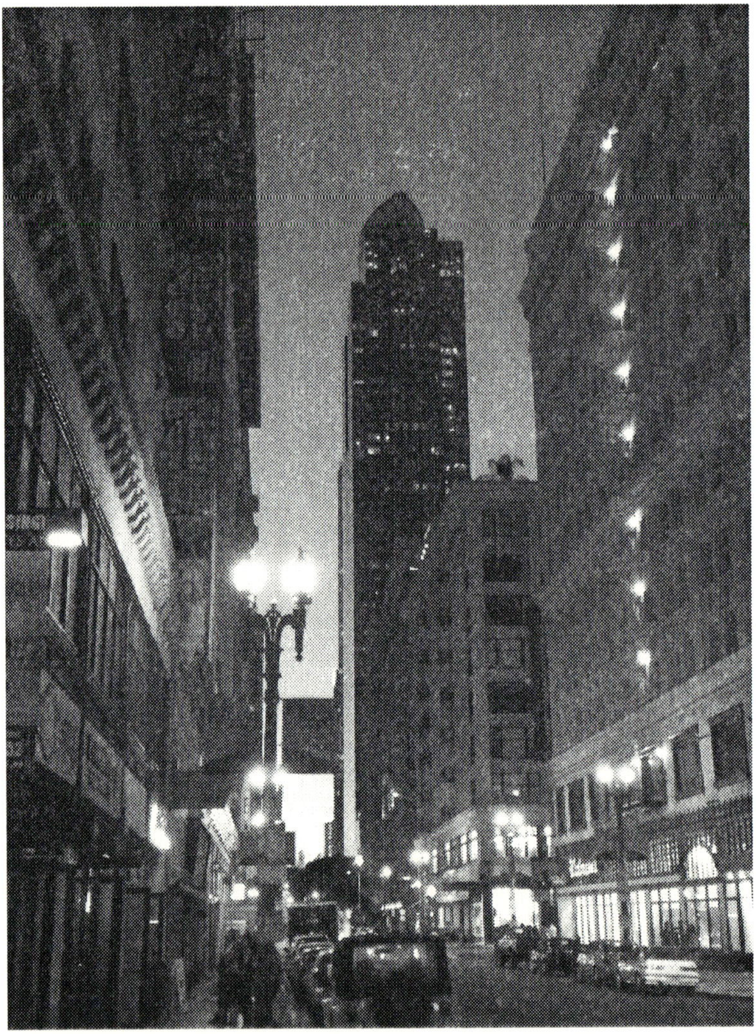

The Seven Stages of Love - An L.A. Haiku-Noir Sequence

the lure
bring your tender love
to the city, 8th floor, the
door's ajar. find me!

the operating instructions
she explicitly
told me how to please her, but
then, she always lied.

the truth
as she walked away
she said, yes, I love women.
I just don't love you.

the rationalization
life's cruel casting call:
I can play taller, blonder,
but I can't play you.

the big missing
if matter cannot
be created or destroyed,
is she still out there?

the acceptance
so tired tonight. you'd
think the bottom had dropped out
of my intentions.

the bullet dodged
deep in my breathing
I stand outside of myself
and see me, breathing.

Author photo by Baz Here

Author Bio

Alexis Rhone Fancher and her husband, Jim, live and work in a loft/studio space in downtown Los Angeles. She is the recipient of multiple Pushcart nominations and a nomination for Best of the Net. Her photographs have been published worldwide. She is poetry editor of *Cultural Weekly*. www.alexisrhonefancher.com

Titles by Sybaritic Press

Demon Under Glass by D.L. Warner
ISBN #0971223203
$11.95
DemonSpawn: On The Run by F.E. Lin, Jenny Saypaw & D.L. Warner
ISBN #978-1607022930
$11.99
L.A. Melange: the first year of poeticdiversity
from the editors of poeticdiversity
ISBN #0971223289
$10.00
Literary Angles: the second year of poeticdiversity
from the editors of poeticdiversity
ISBN #0971223270
$10.00
The Gift of Surrender by D.L. Warner
ISBN #0971223246
$12.95
The Price of Surrender by D.L. Warner
ISBN #9780971223226
$12.95
Nihilistic Foibles by *Marie Lecrivain*
ISBN #9780977867066
$10.00
A Soldier's Choice by D.L. Warner
ISBN #9780977867097
$9.95
A Soldier's Fate by D.L. Warner
ISBN #9781606438466
$11.99
A Soldier's Destiny by D.L. Warner
ISBN #978-1495117282
$12.99
Stories From the Inside Edge by *Brenda Petrakos*
ISBN #09780977867073
$12.00

Seilschaft by Jo Perridge & Cliff Morten
ISBN#9781604613278
$11.99

Naked In Paradise by *Len Richmond*
ISBN #9781604615999
$11.99

Antebellum Messiah by *Marie Lecrivain*
ISBN #9781615319659
$11.00

The Secret Logs of Mistress Janeway by D.L. Warner
Vol. I ISBN #9781450744966
Vol. II ISBN #9781450744973
Vol. III ISBN #9781450744980
$12.95 each

Bitchess by *Marie Lecrivain*
ISBN #9781450789455
$10.00

Ensnared Volume I by D.L. Warner
ISBN #9781450798303
$12.99

Ensnared Volume II by D.L. Warner
ISBN #9781620500743
$12.99

Alternate Lanes by *Marie Lecrivain and the staff of poeticdiversity*
ISBN #9781467546546
$9.95

Love Poems Yes...Really...Love Poems by *Marie Lecrivain*
ISBN #9781467562423
$11.99

From the Four-Chambered Heart edited by *Marie Lecrivain*
ISBN #978-1467581363
$12.95

Diary of the Last Person on Earth by *Robert King*
ISBN #978-1495100420
$12.99

Near Kin edited by *Marie Lecrivain*
ISBN #978-1495105524
$12.99

Diary of the Unnamed Midwife by *Meg Elison*
ISBN #978-1495116360
$11.99